EMB♥DY
Kind
A Guide for Authentic Living

KRISTI TRADER

Featuring: Tisha Marina Bernard, Larissa Czuchnowsky,
Liz Dobbins, Karlie Everhart, Marijo Grogan, Dr. Matt Helm,
Jamison Jacobs, Shaylene King, Mitzi Koors, Sarah Mackay,
Laurie Marshall, Tina Muheim, Krysta O'Neill, Kristin Ray,
Dr. Lisa S Tharler, Jane Ann Trosin, Ari Weinzweig,
Dr. Amy M. Wisner, Blake Zealear

EmbodyKind

Kristi Trader

©Copyright 2022 Kristi Trader

Published by Brave Healer Productions

Paperback ISBN: 978-1-954047-74-7

eBook ISBN: 978-1-954047-73-0

Big love,

Kerlie Everhart xx

Avé Madiol Veneklasen is an artist in love with color and beauty, working primarily as a painter, but who has a strong love of drawing. She was born in Chicago, Illinois, where both of her parents originated. Her father, James Arnold Madiol, is from a long line of Dutch Artists, and his colorful stories inspired Avé from a very young age.

She grew up in New Buffalo, Michigan, where she lived with her mother's Italian extended family in the woods near the shores of Lake Michigan. Later she moved to Grand Rapids, Michigan, where she completed her education at Grand Valley University with a BFA in Fine Art in 1977. She moved to Jackson, Michigan, in 1982. Avé's career has spanned four decades, and during that time, she has been actively creating and exhibiting. She focused primarily on the figure, hosting life drawings weekly in her studio open to students and professional artists. She was also doing Plein air landscape painting during the warmer months. She taught painting at Jackson College as well as doing many workshops and events, in collaboration with artists from other genres, at her studio, Studio DeeplyArt, in Jackson, Michigan.

Most recently, she has relocated to Grass Lake, Michigan, where she has a studio on Little Wolf Lake. Inspired by the incredible beauty all around her, the focus of her work has shifted to primarily landscape, but her love of the feminine figure and its expressiveness continues.

She gives private lessons and hosts exhibits and artists' gatherings, believing that creative collaboration elevates our growth and expands our awareness of the beauty in and all around us.

You can learn more about Avé and find her art at StudioDeeplyArt.com

How long has not good enough
reverberated from my bones
sending an echo to the world
to use and abuse me?

How long have I kept my pain hidden away
afraid that if I unloaded my burdens
I would crush the world with the weight of it all?

Lifetimes
my ancestors whisper to me.

They come to me in my dreams
and haunt my waking moments.
They rattle my rib cage
as I struggle to breathe.

Let it end with you
they whisper again.

I wander around
no clue how to stop it
this pain and self-rejection.
But I am trying to listen
to water.
I'm learning how to nurture
my tiny seed of hope.

Buried
now bursting and open
my ancestors whisper once more
EmbodyKind.

Feel it
in your body
your mind
your soul.
Unload.
Become an expression of love.
Reverberate throughout the world.

Dominique Linden is an EFT practitioner, yoga teacher, and bodyworker. Her main love is writing, and she has spent the past few years sharing her story and insights more than she ever has before. She has deep gratitude for those who share their own struggles so that others might struggle less, and she aspires to be that kind of person as well. In 2018 she awoke to the fact that her depression was not going anywhere, and she was in desperate need of help. Seeing a therapist for the first time, eating better, and practicing yoga regularly changed her life radically. After years of heavy substance use, she found herself able to quit smoking cigarettes, say no to alcohol, and begin the painful process of learning to love herself. Now that she's been living this lifestyle for a while, she has realized a missing ingredient in her life and in many other people's lives. Being kind to oneself. Raised in a household of violence and passed down trauma, the only way she knew how to treat herself was with cruelty. It was how she got through life and got things done with an iron fist. She is very happy to say that is not the case anymore. It is her hope to be an inspiration to others that it is never too late to change how you treat yourself. You can find her writing and services at bitesizedfaith.com.

DISCLAIMER

This book offers health and wellness information and is designed for educational purposes only. You should not rely on this information as a substitute for, nor does it replace professional medical advice, diagnosis, or treatment. If you have any concerns or questions about your physical, mental, or emotional health, you should always consult with a physician or other healthcare professional. Do not disregard, avoid, or delay obtaining medical or health-related advice from your healthcare professional because of something you may have read here. The use of any information provided in this book is solely at your own risk.

Developments in medical research may impact the health advice that appears here. No assurances can be given that the information contained in this book will always include the most relevant findings or developments with respect to the particular material.

Having said all that, know that the experts here have shared their tools, practices, and knowledge with you with a sincere and generous intent to assist you on your health and wellness journey. Please contact them with any questions you may have about the techniques or information they provided. They will be happy to assist you further!

DEDICATION

To those who propelled me to pause and become aware of the need

to become kind to myself as the foundation for kindness to others

as a parent, as a partner, as a co-worker, and as a community member.

I think of you all fondly and am forever grateful

for your leadership, confidence, and grace.

TABLE OF CONTENTS

INTRODUCTION

EmbodyKind is a transformative movement that encourages us all to become an expression of consideration, friendliness, affection, and love.

We're already perfect and whole, just as we are. In every moment, at home, at work, or in our communities, we should all feel free to live authentically as ourselves. Doing so enhances our self-image, establishes trust in relationships, increases our commitment to and satisfaction at work, and creates welcoming and safe communities.

For purposes of this particular volume, co-authors (which I like to call co-stars) were asked to share their stories of how they came to EmbodyKind and to share an applicable practice with the reader.

Open your hearts and minds. You will be welcomed into homes and hear stories of personal development, partnerships, and parenting. You will be welcomed into workplaces and hear stories of leadership development and team building. And, you will be welcomed into schools and hear stories of self-care, student-care, and school-care.

We are here as your guides. We welcome you. Read our stories in whatever order your body, mind, or soul inspires you to do so. This journey is uniquely yours. May the stories inspire you and practices guide you to EmbodyKind in your home, workplace, and community.

With hope that this might just spark a revolution in your body, mind, and soul.

Kristi Trader, MS
Founder: EmbodyKind

CHAPTER 1

THE DISEASE OF NOT GOOD ENOUGH

NAVIGATING THE SYMPTOMS INSIDE AND OUTSIDE OF OUR BODIES

Kristi Trader, MS, Founder: EmbodyKind

MY STORY

I rushed home from work in my mom-mobile, late, like every day—gas on the pedal, eyes in the rearview mirror looking for cops, voice trying to speak over my two boys on the other line of the cell phone. I pulled into the driveway with the expectation that everything should run smoothly. I gave clear instructions. But, alas, I'd always find something wrong. Just as I was programmed, nothing was ever good enough.

I walked in with the bag of work I needed to complete that evening. The dog was panting and slobbering all over my work clothes, and nothing I asked for was completed. The boys were not dressed for soccer. Nothing was out to cook for dinner. I peeked at their folders from school; no homework was done between when the bus dropped them off and when I got home from work.

I took a deep breath, threw something frozen in a pan, and yelled at the boys, "Go get dressed for soccer!" It wasn't minutes, and they were fighting over whose clothes were whose. I swore we labeled all of them. I went to break up the fight. While I was in the back of the house, their dad came home and asked, "What's burning?" *Awesome! I must not have put any water in the pan. Oops.*

I pitched the dinner into the sink. I got the boys into the car without their cleats on. They would have to figure that out while I took them through a disgusting drive-thru. It was the only option between home and the soccer field. They were late, and their cleats still weren't on. They limped to the field through freshly rained-on grass. I didn't get to change, so my heels dug, one-by-one, into the soft mud. I bent down to get one of their cleats tied, and Dad got the other one. "You're late. Give me five laps!" The coaches were thrilled.

Everyone finally got situated, the kids on their bench ready to start their game and their dad and I on the sideline ready to watch the game. Then my pager went off. Yes, one of those ancient things. I walked back through the mud so I didn't distract the parents watching the game, my heels, one-by-one, going in and out of the grass, and I called the number. It was my boss. She had a question about an excel spreadsheet. *Are you kidding me? A spreadsheet?* While excel can be my superpower, I worked for a hospital, I'm not a cardiologist. *Why was she paging me? Those things are for emergencies. Why did I even carry one?*

This was a recurring evening in our home, and I thought,

If only my boss could have work set up so I could leave on time.

If only the boys could be dressed.

If only the boys could take something out for dinner.

If only the boys could have their clothes laid out and know whose is whose.

If only their dad could be home from work sooner.

If only their dad could throw something on for dinner.

If only their coach could start practice or games later.

If only my boss didn't call me when I was with my family.

I had an "if only" for everyone but myself because, beyond my spreadsheets, I truly felt like I was saving lives. Maybe not like the cardiologist. But, here's what I knew at the time: one-third to one-half of life satisfaction is derived directly from workplace wellbeing, engagement, and happiness. The assumption then is that more engaged and happy employees would yield community members, and thus communities, with greater levels of life satisfaction: happier people and communities.

My work was in organizational development. Specifically, one of my primary responsibilities was to develop and facilitate a curriculum to improve staff engagement results. I was seeing people's lives, families, work teams, and a community change. I told my boss, "When I facilitate these workshops, it's not uncommon for people to cry." She'd look at me strangely, shake her head, and state that she just couldn't understand why. "What in the curriculum would possibly bring about this reaction?"

And then, she attended one of the workshops and experienced the first activity we did to build trust. We sat in a circle and, for the first time, people who work in a team were asked to respond to questions I modified from the book, *Five Dysfunctions of a Team:* 1) Where did you grow up? 2) Tell us about your home life growing up: parents, siblings, where did you fall in order? 3) What was the most challenging thing about your childhood? 4) What is something unique about you?

By the time we got to question two, someone was crying, and my boss offered the staff member one of her special tissues. People had one, never been asked these questions at work, and two, never experienced someone listening as though they cared.

I loved my work so much, and I saw it changing people's lives. But I observed, in my department and in myself, that we were not walking the talk we promoted to the rest of our workplace. That ate at my soul. I should be clear, this was not uncommon. This is just one story of every place I worked up until this point.

Dr. Gabor Mate, author of *When the Body Says No: Exploring the Stress-Disease Connection,* says, "If you don't know how to say no, your body will say it for you." Dr. Mate's 11-hour *Masterclass for Healers* was integral to defining my practices I'll share in this chapter. His understanding and approach to the body-mind-soul connection are unlike any other medical doctor I have yet to learn from.

My body was saying no, and I felt it everywhere inside and outside of my body: physically, emotionally, and relationally. I thought the answer would come from everywhere except myself because I was raised to be a "Yes!" woman, an extra-credit doer, a faithful volunteer, the classroom mom, send an extra dozen for the bake sale (okay, that never really happened), make a meal for the neighbor who had surgery, etc., all while working full-time and raising two boys.

I'm not sure our team ever did this exercise. But if we had, here's what they would have learned about me. I grew up in Brownstown, Michigan. I'm the daughter of Curt and Laurie Biro, who remain married. I'm the oldest of three, and we all fit social psychologists' definition of birth order and personality; the oldest: me, the middle: Curt, and the youngest: Kari.

The most challenging thing about my childhood was the disease of not-good-enough: part of being the oldest child and part of ancestral wounds. Oldest children are dominant and conscientious. We want things done now and right. Firstborns tend to be overachievers, and Dr. Michelle P. Maiden, a child, and family therapist, notes, "[We] often have an intense fear of failure, so nothing [we] accomplish feels good enough." This is often passed down in families traumatically and unconsciously.

It started in first grade. I anxiously awaited my turn to get the envelope. I opened it quickly, did a scan, and my heart dropped. I wanted to cry. But, we weren't a crying family. I think it showed weakness. So, I threw the envelope in my backpack, put my coat on, and lined up to be dismissed and walk home.

The 0.8-mile walk home felt like an eternity. My palms were sweaty, and I walked with a pout, grinding my teeth. I'm sure my cheeks were red, my heart was beating out of my chest, and my mind was swirling with all of the thoughts of what I could have done differently. I walked through the door and threw the envelope on the counter. My mom opened it, scanned it just like I did, and her first question was, "What is this?" pointing to the only B on my first-grade report card. She was given the disease of not-good-enough by also being the oldest child and through ancestral wounds. My smart ass said, "It's the second letter of the alphabet." This is the foundation of the disease that has wracked my body, mind, and soul for decades.

Being that I contracted the disease in elementary school, the symptoms showed up very young and progressed rapidly. That same year, in first grade, I was given a nickname from a boy in my class because I have asthma and cough a lot: "Mucus." By third grade, I was taken out of my regular classes to participate in advanced classes. I was also labeled "talented" and "gifted." This perpetuated nights of falling asleep repeating facts and figures. But I wasn't alone. I vividly remember a figure that looked like the Grim Reaper at the foot of my bed each night. He did nothing more than stand there. But still, he tortured me, at least through my college years. So, of course, I didn't sleep well, and I'd wake up frazzled. I would be sick about the content of the day because an A- meant I didn't get an A like everyone else in the group. In this group, we all had this mindset. These were my first bouts of anxiety at eight years old!

By fourth grade, I couldn't balance academic achievement and friends, and my friend group started to leave me out. In fifth grade, I contracted mononucleosis. Sixth grade was my favorite, yet I had to work harder than I had ever worked because there was a competition every week, and I'd be damned if I was going to lose. What this disease defined is that results, not relationships, were most important to me because recognition was essential to my self-worth and wellbeing.

Another part of this disease is losing time. For example, other than being bullied and constant body image self-talk, most of the seventh through twelfth grade is a blur. Part goes back to the nickname and the friend group leaving me out. I didn't want to participate in life because of the way I was treated, so my memories are very few. One, though, is very vivid and the reason for the work I do today. The boy that gave me the nickname, back in first grade, started a chant at an athletic event with his crew of buddies, every one whose name I remember till this day. They were chanting, "Mucus sucks." The next day, he came to my locker and said, "See ya later, Mucus," and gave me a hug. All of this was very strange because we did not speak with one another, and we definitely did not hug one another. The next day I learned that he was found dead. He died by suicide.

I continued damaging behaviors to extremes through my higher education and into my career, marriage, and parenting. Those stories will be told in future volumes. Then I learned about the spoon theory. The spoon theory is a visual representation of the mental and physical energy a person has in a period of time to complete activities that can only be replaced by rest. It was developed when Christine Miserandino was at a restaurant with her friend and was asked, "What is it like to have a chronic illness?" Christine gathered all the spoons around her and explained to her friend, "While people without chronic illness have unlimited spoons, people with chronic illness start each day with a limited number of spoons and must choose wisely how to spend them."

As someone with chronic illnesses, I was not choosing how to spend my spoons wisely. When we were kids, these stressors in our bodies looked like headaches or stomach aches. But, when we get older, we have more amazing body parts that have developed for stress to attack. The list of my diagnoses was absurd. I was falling apart at 32, and there was more to come. But, I was also not being kind to myself, my body, mind, soul, children, husband, co-workers, workplace, or community. I'm sure the list went on. Do I believe every medical diagnosis was stress related? No. But do I believe I was unhealthy because I continued to expose myself to stress? Yes.

As I was experiencing the strong pangs of my body saying *no* to my work, I was given an amazing opportunity to make a drastic change for myself and my family. What I initially thought I was being asked to do was an evening or weekend commitment that would've looked good on my resume. But, what I was actually being asked to do, was a part-time contract which would require that I quit the full-time job that was making me sick.

I thought there was no way possible I could commit, mostly for financial reasons. But, when I was given the offer, it was only $3,000 less than I was making working full-time. I would've been stupid to say no. I was given an opportunity to become aware of and evaluate my ability to EmbodyKind. And then, through intense self-care, therapy, and seeking deep education, I was able to understand family constellations, be a witness to my own story and stressors, and work through the practices I'll share with you in this chapter. I have developed them to be a recipe for success in advocating kindness for yourself as the foundation for kindness to others as a parent, partner, co-worker, and as a community member.

THE PRACTICE

Below I have outlined the step-by-step recipe of practices I've developed to help subdue the symptoms of the disease of not-good-enough. I set aside time for these practices regularly. None of them are something you simply do once and never return to. I have intentionally only expanded on the main practice in this volume, as my upcoming works will expand on the others.

Best wishes as you explore! I hope you find as much relief as I have.

EmbodyKind,

Kristi Trader, MS
Founder: EmbodyKind

One of the most climactic experiences of my life thus far was a workshop with John Wineland and Kendra Cunov, *The Art of Loving Fiercely.* This led me to intensive work with Genivieve and Jaiya. These experiences are where I found my*self* beyond psychology and theory and into the realm of practice. It's where the finishing touches of my own remedy and prescription were developed.

The ultimate practice of **EmbodyKind** requires that you learn to know where you are at in space right now, not past or future, present. Only through this practice can you be available for kindness in the present moment. Willa Blythe Baker says,

> One of the most important wisdoms is that the body lives in the here and now. The body brings us into the present moment, while the mind is running around with its stories. The mind dives into the past and anticipates the future. It's worrying about this and trying to fix that. The thinking mind is the agitated part of our experience, while the body is centered in the here and now.

To open our body, mind, and soul to the present moment, we have to think:

a. What is happening around me?

This is exteroception; what is happening on the exterior of you. Exteroception is the five senses we typically think of: sight, sound, smell, touch, and taste.

b. Where is my body in space?

This is proprioception, also known as kinesthesia. Proprioception in its most basic sense is body awareness: knowing where your body parts are, coordinating body parts and senses, and knowing how much force to use.

c. What is happening inside my body?

This is interoception: what is happening inside of you. Interoception is the nervous system processing internal organ function and autonomic nervous system activity, including emotion, across conscious and unconscious levels.

To continue this practice with an interactive meditation, visit my website at: KristiTrader.com/Books

Other ingredients in the recipe to EmbodyKind that will be discussed in future volumes include:

1. Get to know thyself. The foundation of my healing and my work with any of my clients is the ancient Greek aphorism, "Know thyself." Brené Brown says,

   Our connection with other people is only as solid and deep as our connection to ourselves. In order for me to be connected to you, I have to know who I am. I have to be connected to myself. And, I think, what we end up doing, is we end up desperately searching for connection with other people, when we have no idea who we are.

2. Meditate and reflect. Find time to be still. Prioritize this time. This time will look different for everyone. Meditation means different things for different people. It has meant different things at different times for myself. Meditation and reflection don't have to be alone. There's power in numbers and intention. C.S. Lewis says, "Friendship is born at that moment when one person says to another: 'What! You too? I thought I was the only one.'"

3. Use a coach and or therapist regularly. Even as a coach, I'm constantly surrounding myself with other coaches and therapists for support and advice. Sometimes this is individual work. Other times this is in a group setting. All of us need neutral parties to help guide and direct us. None of us have ever arrived or are free from needing a helping hand. Matthew Kelly says,

No woman becomes great on her own. The people around them help to make them great. We all need people in our lives who raise our standards, remind us of our essential purpose, and challenge us to become the best version of ourselves.

EmbodyKind. Bring your body, mind, and soul into the present moment. Know what is happening around you; be aware of your senses. Feel where your body is in space; know how to use it. Sense what is happening inside your body; process the conscious and unconscious. And, finally, practice regularly. John Wineland says,

> Self-expression is actually a muscle that needs to be exercised. And, part of learning the artistry of love is learning to express various things through your body, through your heart. If, for some reason, you were not celebrated as a child in the expression of your truth through your heart, your body will clamp down and not express things you feel or want to express. So you have to create space to 'clear the pipes' and express those unfelt emotions. We all get into a habit of the things we're okay expressing. The things we aren't okay expressing, but feel anyway, get stuck in our bodies. Then we cannot be fully available because we have knots of unfelt feelings. Creating a regular practice of self-expression will exercise that muscle and make you more available for love.

This recipe can be framed for however you need to approach the method at any given time. For example, you can use it to:

Help subdue the symptoms of the disease of not-good-enough.

Or, you can use it to:

Find success in advocating kindness for yourself as the foundation for kindness to others as a parent, as a partner, as a co-worker, and as a community member.

Be present. Meet the moment with authenticity and vulnerability. Find your*self*. Be open to EmbodyKind.

Kristi Trader designs custom experiences for all ages with the intent of embodying kindness in ourselves, others, and our communities. EmbodyKind is a transformative movement that encourages us all to become an expression of consideration, friendliness, affection, and love.

She believes that we are already perfect and whole, just as we are. In every moment, at home, at work, or in our communities, we should all feel free to live authentically as ourselves. Doing so enhances our self-image, establishes trust in relationships, increases our commitment to and satisfaction at work, and creates welcoming and safe communities.

She uses an integrated approach, including personality profiling, communication tools, storytelling, embodiment practices, and play. In her years of experience, she has facilitated personal and relational development, workplace engagement, bullying prevention, restorative practices, and community building services to diverse industries, including education, finance, government, healthcare, spiritual, and technology.

Kristi graduated summa cum laude from Concordia University with a Master of Science in Organizational Leadership and Administration. She also holds a Bachelor of Arts in Organizational Management from Spring Arbor University and an Associate of Arts from North Central University. She has written for Elephant Journal and Tattooed Buddha.

Connect with Kristi:

Email: info@KristiTrader.com

Website: https://KristiTrader.com

Facebook: https://www.Facebook.com/KristiTrader

Twitter: https://www.Twitter.com/KristiTrader

Instagram: https://www.Instagram.com/KristiTrader

LinkedIn: https://www.LinkedIn.com/in/KristiTrader

Bibliography

Brown, Brené, director. "The Language of Emotion and Human Experience." *Atlas of The Heart,* season 1, episode 1, Brené Brown, 2022.

Kelly, Matthew. *The Rhythm of Life: Living Every Day with Passion and Purpose.* Blue Sparrow Books, 2015.

Kiesling, Stephen, and Willa Baker. "How to Embody Kindness." *Spirituality & Health,* https://www.spiritualityhealth.com/how-to-embody-kindness. Accessed 26 April 2022.

Lencioni, Patrick M. *The Five Dysfunctions of a Team: A Leadership Fable.* Wiley, 2002.

Lewis, Clive Staples. *The Four Loves.* Harcourt, Brace, 1960.

Mate, Gabor. *When the Body Says No: Exploring the Stress-Disease Connection.* Wiley, 2011.

"The Spoon Theory written by and spoken by Christine Miserandino." *YouTube,* 16 December 2010, https://www.youtube.com/watch?v=jn5IBsm49Rk. Accessed 14 April 2022.

Voo, Jocelyn, and Michelle Maidenberg. "Birth Order Traits: Your Guide to Sibling Personality Differences." Parents, 30 July 2020, https://www.parents.com/baby/development/social/birth-order-and-personality/. Accessed 27 April 2022.

Wineland, John. "Exercising the Muscle of Self-Expression." Facebook, 2020, https://fb.watch/cGws6nHYB0/. Accessed 28 April 2022.

Wineland, John, and Cunov Kendra. "The Art of Loving Fiercely Online Immersion — John Wineland." John Wineland, https://www.johnwineland.com/the-art-of-loving-fiercely-online-immersion-2021. Accessed 25 April 2022.

CHAPTER 2

SITTING IN YOUR SHIT

AN AWARENESS PRACTICE FOR RADICAL ACCEPTANCE

Mitzi Koors, Intuitive, Healer, Seer

MY STORY

I'm in search of an end to suffering. I wander through the noise in search of stillness, a place where the vibrating stops and I can be.

I sit currently at my computer, listening to my beautiful, almost six-year-old son hollering my name from outside the window. We went together to feed Coco and Poppy, our two cows, and the perfect opportunity allowed for my escape. My butt will remain planted in this seat until, eventually, he will find me and continue the stream of questions and assessments of the world as they come to him. We're at around 47,924 today.

It's these moments when I'd give about anything for a cave of my own. The part of me who knows how to find my stillness (let's call her Irene) is tied up tight with a heavy piece of duct tape over her mouth. Irene and I lock eyes, but I'm a bit resentful for her lack of participation before we've gotten to this point. She's sweet and seems to get pushed around easily, so I leave her be and stew over the condition I'm temporarily comfortable occupying. If she weren't tied up, I'm sure she'd ask, "Have you meditated today?" And then patiently wait for me to answer the question she already knew the answer to. Her willingness to be still while I come to my own conclusions is painfully kind.

Irene would then allow a reveal of the state of my body, which would again confirm the absence of the morning meditation. I feel jittery. My consciousness hangs out about two inches above my physical body and another couple of feet out front. The front half of my body feels tugged forward, and the back half and my insides feel like scratchy oatmeal. I notice an orange ball taking up most of the inside of my head. It's firm, shiny, plastic-like, and fairly dense. This doesn't feel so good.

Control your external space, and you can control your internal space, he rages. In my space today, among other voices, is one that sounds like my dad. When he's at the podium, the rest of my parts stand at attention, including Irene, who cringes at the tantrum. Irene has compassion for the pain others must be experiencing to discharge that energy through others. We all stand back and watch the critic, the child, and the peacemaker.

When the raging father breaks his stride, another sees an opportunity to cut in. The critic begins hurling insults and accusations overhand with the full force of an MLB pitcher. *You've had therapy for this, paid thousands of dollars, walked through hell, and he's still here?* Although the critic works independently, he holds the rest of us out of the way so both he and Dad can speak. They're like peanut butter and jelly.

This place, in this seat, with the cacophony of voices, energies, and sensations running through me, I'm grateful. I'm seeing my shit. Sitting right in it with them. I'm looking them straight in the eye, holding space for them to talk back. I'm giving them a voice to speak their truth, pulling it out of the dark recesses of the moldy basement. *What do you want from me?* They want what we all want: to be seen, validated, and set free.

In her podcast, Radical Acceptance - Gateway to Love, Wisdom, and Peace, Tara Brach summarizes a story of the Buddha and one of many of his encounters with Mara during his lifetime. Mara represents greed, hatred, delusion, and all the shadowy parts of ourselves we don't like. One afternoon while speaking to a crowd in a field, Mara is sneaking around in the back of the gathering. The Buddha's attendant Ananda saw Mara, got nervous, and went to tell the Buddha, afraid Mara would disrupt the day. But the Buddha said, "No worries," and he went directly to Mara and said, "I see you, Mara. Let's have tea."

Buddha didn't elevate or demonize Mara. It was simply an invitation to sit together and have tea. Being with someone allows you to hear their tone of voice, see the twitch in body language, and the way the eyes move with the ebb and flow of the conversation. This isn't the time to react or make decisions about what you'll do in the future, but to be fully present. Listen. Watch. Be a neutral observer.

Today I'm inviting my shit to tea. Today, at this moment, Dad's voice is settling down. Replacing the bracing tension are heavy cotton clouds in my arms and shoulders. It feels like a hug that never happened. I'm sad for my younger self sitting shivering in the corner. The girl shrinks and watches the anger in paralysis. I see her. I see him. I am neither.

I have space here, in my arms, for her to see me. I'm an adult now, and I can take care of her. She needn't be afraid. She is loved.

I have space here, in my head, for him to see me too. For him to know I appreciate his protection from the world that was a threat to my small heart. He is valued.

As rage softens to sadness laced with frustration, I melt and vibrate simultaneously. Still seeking a rapid remedy so I can open my heart to this little boy who can't wait to share his world with me, I feel the frustration.

I remember the words of Kristin Neff in her book Self-Compassion, "This is a moment of suffering. Suffering is part of life. May I be kind to myself in this moment. May I give myself the compassion I need."

Through time and circumstance, our parts are formed. When I look at them independently and discover the places they inhabit in my body, I notice there are many holding their own vibrations, triggers, relationships, perspectives, and goals. They work with each other, most of the time in recognizable patterns and responses, all with a single goal: to protect me. When these energies made a home in my space, it was based on a story told by my environment. I accepted that story, and it became my own. Through the years, there have been many.

One sunny, beautiful September afternoon in 1986, I rode shotgun in my mom's orange 1975 Pontiac Astre. Madonna was on the radio, and I was belting Material Girl with the passion of 1,000 tweens. I had every lyric down, and the scene came complete with my own lace gloves. In the back seat was my best friend, Tracy. She sang with the same fervor, and through the open windows, we spilled our pre-teen lust for diamonds, pearls, and boys.

Tracy had a background singing at church. She followed every note and pitch change, and her timing was on point. Until this day, I admired her ability to hang with the best pop songs, and that was the extent of our differences as far as I was concerned. I had my place, and she had hers, right beside me.

We were serenading each passing neighborhood that day, and it felt amazing. Then from the back seat, Tracy says, "Let's have a contest. Who's the better singer?" I was game. Mom was the judge. We took down the last of the chorus and waited for the results. "Tracy's the winner. Singing isn't your thing." Mom reported. All three of us laughed. I stopped singing.

Now, I'm certain I wasn't headed for Star Search, but I felt alive singing. I could occupy space. My dad's verbal abuse kept me small inside, though. It no longer felt safe. This picture made a home in my body and continued to remind me that the outside, and the people who were safe to me, didn't approve.

Inside, today in this seat, this part still lives. The energy has changed shape over the years, but that voice is still part of my choir. The Madonna wannabe who wants to shrink, and he who wants to rage and consume, live together here. We're still having tea.

THE PRACTICE

Seeing our parts is taking into your conscious mind that which is in your space. About three feet away from your physical body is your bubble. Everything outside of your bubble is not you, and what is in your bubble should only be you. Inside your bubble, your spirit is made perfectly for your body. The DNA is written for you—only you. This "you" vibration is the space held when you're truly feeling yourself. If the voice is self-deprecating, critical, judgmental, or ego-driven, it's not you.

Intuition is simply awareness. What do you feel arising? When your intuitive radio is tuned in to your body, what do you notice? When you're tuned into a room, what do you feel? When you're tuned into the person in front of you, what sensations begin in your space? The energy in and around you can reveal itself through pictures, feeling, knowing, smelling, tasting, and hearing. We all have the radio. You get to decide whether to turn it on and peruse the stations.

Here's a fun exercise you can do to get your radio fired up. We do this at home a lot when making decisions. My 23-year-old son loves to use this tool when deciding which restaurant to go to for dinner.

Take out a sheet of paper and cut it into three to four equal sizes according to how many options are presented. Write one option on each piece of paper. Fold each in half and mix them up. Take a moment to breathe, come into your body and relax. Close your eyes. For more clarity, do the meditation below first. Take each piece of paper one at a time into your hands. Don't try to guess which is which (this causes performance pressure and will shut you down). Instead, notice which images, feelings, thoughts, or sensations come to mind? What is the vibration of that piece of paper? Draw or write that on the paper. Do the same for each. When you've finished, look at them.

CLAIMING YOUR SPACE

Most mornings, after the frenzy of hair combing, teeth brushing and finding lost shoes before the school rush, I have time to sit for a few moments. Typically, at the beginning of the day, the voices are hushed. The cacophony of shoulds from parents, friends, and Instagram hasn't yet overcome the centered me I know should be calling the shots in here. There's less to compete with to find my voice here. I take time to clear what's not mine, reconstitute what is me back into my space and ground out what might come in through the day before it becomes lodged.

Sometimes my morning meditation happens in my favorite desk chair, on occasion in the car in the parking lot at work, and many times on the toilet. The commode is the perfect spot to be left alone for a few minutes. Find your opportunity when life presents it. Don't wait until life clears a space for you. It won't.

Once you find your spot, close your eyes. Take a deep breath in, then release it. Find your body. Become aware of the center of your own head. Bring all your awareness, your consciousness, into that space. Imagine the center of your headspace is a grassy meadow in a clearing between forests, with a large blanket spread out for you. You're sitting on that blanket, taking in your surroundings. Look around that meadow, and see if there's anyone else there frolicking, chatting, or perhaps sitting on your blanket with you, affecting your space. Notice the weather, the phase of the sun or moon, and if there's a breeze. If there are people in your meadow, kindly invite them to leave. Imagine those people walking to the edge of the meadow and disappearing into the forest. Once the last person leaves your meadow, visualize the long grasses becoming still, calming down, and coming to complete stillness. See yourself sitting in the calmest, quietest meadow you can possibly imagine. If you see any pollution in the air, clouds, or fog, see a clean, warm breeze blowing through your meadow, sweeping away anything that keeps your airspace from being clear and pristine. Now that your meadow is all cleaned out and still, see yourself in the middle of that soft blanket in the grass. Decide that you're going to do the rest of this meditation from the center of your own clear head.

See down from your center of the head, through your body toward the earth. Visualize a grounding cord as wide as your hips. The material can be whatever you like, a tree trunk, a pipe, whatever feels right to you. The cord has an airtight seal and goes straight down into the center of the earth. Once it's connected, let your body release. Release everything in your body that isn't yours. Imagine that energy falling out of your body and right down that grounding cord. All that ick and yuck leaving your space and falling deep into the earth to be healed and sent back to its original owner. Once you set the cord, it will remain the rest of the day.

Create a big golden sun above your head at least three times the size of your body. Place a big magnet in that sun, and with your intention, use that big magnet to call back all of your energy from wherever it might be in time and space. Imagine your energy zooming from all sorts of directions, back to that sun. Visualize that sun filling up with your energy. And once you've collected up all your energy, and are completely full of you, have that sun bring your energy to the highest vibration possible for your body. Imagine that the sun is vibrantly bright and shimmering. Then pop that sun and watch the warm gold, soft light flow down into your body, filling your toes, legs, belly, chest, arms, and up into your head. Be filled completely with your own energy. Notice how that feels when you have all your energy in your body. Enjoy this space for a while. This is you.

Finding stillness and a pure voice that's yours is a beautiful gift to yourself. Cultivate this as often as you're able. Humans have a large spectrum of potential experiences, and this is a gift. We navigate strategically, float vulnerably, and paddle frantically through our internal and external environments. Returning to our voice, in neutrality and amusement, is a cloudless sky in a paddleboat on a summer day. Nowhere to be, no *who* to be. You sit.

About a year ago, I did a deep house energy cleansing after the build of our home. I grounded it, wiped it clean, and cleared all the grungy things brought in from the outside. The ceiling in our home is natural wood shiplap with lots of natural knots and a clear finish. Toward the end of my meditation, I noticed up on our ceiling hundreds of small lights. Tiny tree-dwelling beings were brought in from the harvest of the wood. I healed them, thanked them, and sent them back to the outside, where they could occupy a living space. I slept wonderfully that night and woke to a warm and messy-haired four-year-old joining me for a morning snuggle. After getting comfortable under the soft covers, he looked up at the ceiling for quite some time. When a few moments passed, I said, "What's the matter, buddy? What do you see?" He said, "Mamma, before when I used to look up at the ceiling, I would see things looking back at me. Today, they're all gone. Where are they?" I snuggled him close and said, "I saw them and healed them, love. Now they are free."

Mitzi came to this life with a decision to feel and see over the spectrum of what makes us human: compassion, loneliness, elation, creativity, bitterness, love, jealousy, and pure joy. She chose this life to see.

When Mitzi was a little girl, she noticed she was very aware of the way spaces felt when she entered them. Her body reacted with sensations that told the story of the lingering energy in the room. People without language share similar stories, and Mitzi knew at a young age that communicating beyond the physical is our spirit's first language. Our energetic bodies share all the things our voices don't.

Mitzi became Reiki certified (I, II, and Reiki Master) six years ago, and she started noticing pictures energetic bodies were sharing, not just sensations. She completed the Enlightenment Program at the Boulder Psychic Institute. BPI has equipped her with tools to see and heal by clearing energy from bodies and spaces. Mitzi now offers aura and chakra healings, energy and past life readings, as well as courses on intuition development.

The other parts of her, Mitzi's a wife and mother of three and has had what feels like full lifetimes in the fields of archaeology, anthropology, art, sculpture, design, sustainability, marketing renewable energy, and organic farming. Mitzi and her husband, Brent, homestead 38 acres and recently built a strawbale home. It's a simple, quiet, and beautifully fulfilling life that has given her the opportunity to sit, be still and listen to the vibrations of life.

Connect with Mitzi:

Website: https://ikshana-see.com

Facebook: https://www.Facebook.com/MitziKoors

Instagram: https://www.Instagram.com/ikshana.see

Instagram: https://www.Instagram.com/fullflowerfarm

CHAPTER 3

CULTIVATING KINDNESS IN GIRL WORLD

INTERACTIVE JOURNALING TO SPARK CONFIDENCE

Shaylene King, Founder: The Mean Girl Extinction Project

MY STORY

"Mom! You've got to see this!" My daughter Jordan shouted as she stormed through the front door. She pulled me toward our family computer and logged onto her Facebook account.

"You're not going to believe what these mean girls did to Abby!"

She scrolled through her feed and clicked on a video. I watched in horror as two girls sat on a bed and told intimate scathing lies about Abby as they laughed into the camera. The worst part? They posted it to a boy's Facebook account, knowing he rarely checked it, so it would do a lot of damage before he noticed it and took it down.

"Mom, we've got to help her." Jordan pleaded as tears fell from her face. "Absolutely not!" I blurted. "I don't want you to be these girls' next victim."

Jordan looked at me with the most hurtful expression on her face.

"But you've always told me to stand up for those who are being mistreated."

Her words hit me hard. She was right! Being kind and standing up for someone being picked on has been one of the most important messages as a parent I have tried to instill and model with my kids and here I was telling her not to help her friend. For the next few hours, we sat side by side on the piano bench in front of the family computer and discussed how to best help her friend. Our online search began by looking up everything we could find on relational aggression, a type of girl bullying. We were shocked to realize there was not a lot of information or resources specific to relational aggression out there, so we decided to become that resource! Through assemblies, workshops, and community outreach, Jordan and I worked together to make girl world a safer place to live.

As I became an expert in understanding relational aggression between girls, the common thread leading to mistreatment was insecurity. I call it "insecuri-TEEN." Although we were not able to stop the "mean" girl behavior from hurting Jordan's friend in 2014, we have since found ways to prevent relational aggression from happening to other girls.

I will *never* forget that moment and the way Jordan looked at me. It's a moment I most regret and a moment I'm most thankful for, as it changed the trajectory of my work as an educator. It was from this moment, back in 2014, that *The Mean Girl Extinction Project* (TMGEP) was founded to abolish the "mean girl" mentality, and our mission to help cultivate a community of kindness in girl world was born.

After working with thousands of girls in over 100 schools since 2014, I can confidently say meanness in girl world is deeply rooted in insecurity—Every. Single. Time. Research shows insecurity begins to rear its ugly head for girls as young as eight and is at its highest in middle school. These middle school years are when a girl's body begins to develop, hormones are raging out of control, and she is trying to figure out *who* she is and *what* her place is in the world. Insecurity, if not managed, can be used as a weapon of mass destruction in girl world. This weapon of insecurity was used on Jordan's friend all those years ago, and insecurity continues to be a ticking time bomb affecting girl world now.

Being a girl and trying to navigate girl world can be tough. It can be even tougher as a parent, guardian, educator, and mentor trying to figure out *how* to support them.

One of the best ways I've found to help traverse this stage in a girl's life is to provide options that allow them the opportunity to do the work and figure it out for themselves. Not an easy thing to do. Our natural instinct is to fix it. So then, how do you equip and empower girls to do the work themselves? I'm glad you asked!

Interactive journaling is a powerful tool you can use to help girls EmbodyKind by managing their insecurity, building confidence, and positively navigating girl world. Through guided prompts, activities, and calls to action, interactive journaling provides girls the opportunity to better understand who they are, practice self-love, and promote positive emotional health through self-discovery. When a girl has a stronger cognizance around who she is and feels more confident in her skin, she is more likely to be a positive influence. This positive influence will help her cultivate a community of kindness in her circle of girl world.

There are excellent interactive journals for girls available for purchase on sites such as Amazon (I will be giving you a free chapter from one of my interactive journals called *Girl Tough, Identity*), but you can create your own for home or school. What I love about interactive journaling—the topics of discussion are limitless. Struggling with body image? Or maybe it's comparing themselves to others? Frame your journaling around things related to the issue they're dealing with.

THE PRACTICE

Here are six parts of interactive journaling I use to spark confidence and EmbodyKind. (I'll be using snippets from my interactive journal *Girl Tough, Identity* to share as examples for each section.)

Let's Talk About It - Kick off the topic you want to work through. This is your teaching piece. What do you want them to learn? What is the take-away? Keep it clear, concise, and bite-sized. I keep it within one page.

Did you know the friends you choose can hugely influence the person you become? They can impact your values, affect your attitudes and influence the decisions you make. So, it goes without saying (but I'll say it anyway), it's super important to choose your friends wisely!

My cheer coach once said, "Tell me who your friends are, and I will tell you who you are." Her point was this: if you choose friends who are kind, inclusive, and encouraging, you will likely also be kind, inclusive, and encouraging. But the same can also be true if your friends are insecure, unkind, and gossipers; you will probably find yourself to be insecure, unkind, and a gossip. Funny how that works, huh? Unfortunately, I learned this the hard way. In middle school, I traded my two good friends to be part of the cool crowd—The. Worst. Year. Ever! My new friends were toxic. Gossiping, backstabbing, and girl drama was rampant, and I fully participated in all of it. By the summer, I had developed low self-esteem and poor body image, and my insecurity was off the hook. I went from being happy and positive to negative, angry, and untrusting. What changed? The answer is simple. When you spend time with your friends, their behavior, values, and attitudes can rub off on you. The question is, what's actually rubbing off on you? Does it positively or negatively influence you? The truth is, friends will influence you. The good news is, you get to decide who your friends are and how they will influence you.

Get into It - This section is designed to activate what was read. Practice activities will help put pen to paper to connect with what was just learned in *Let's Talk About It.* I love to insert graphics or clipart as part of these activities to increase interaction and enrich visual learning. You can check out the free chapter I'll be sharing with you at the end to see how I used interactive graphics for the activities below.

Thermometer

Take the temperature of your friendships. Are they keeping you healthy or making you sick?

Friendship Venn Diagram

Sometimes it can help to see things laid out in front of you. Compare your friends with each other! Is one healthier than the other? Or compare yourself with a friend. What are your differences? What do you have in common?

Go Deeper - Curated journal prompts help process what was learned and practiced in the above sections. Prompts should not be able to be answered with a "yes" or "no." Instead, they should encourage looking inward and digging deep.

Look at yourself in the mirror. What kind of friend is staring back at you? How can you be a better friend?

Write about the history of one of your friendships. Include: How did you meet, why did you choose them as a friend, what do you do for fun, how do you resolve conflicts, and what do you wish for your friendship?

Refer to your Friend-Venn; let's unpack it. Do you have any negative friendships in your life right now that you realize are not good for you? What is it that makes them unhealthy for you? Are they worth saving? or do you need to think about letting them go?

You Go Girl - This is my favorite piece! I refer to it as a to-do list of challenges. These challenges are practical applications to put what they have worked through into actionable steps. One of the best ways to build confidence and EmbodyKind is to take them out of their "me" obsessed world where the focus is all about them. This gives them the chance to take a break and shift their focus to thinking about and serving others. Serving others not only builds confidence but promotes self-esteem. Helping others releases oxytocin, serotonin, and dopamine in the brain, boosting their mood and thwarting cortisol, the stress hormone. Here are a few challenges on friendship.

July 30th is International Friendship Day! Send a card, "old school" through the mail to your friends and tell them what you appreciate about them.

Create a positive song playlist and share it with your friends.

Go out of your way this week to be a good friend. Send an encouraging text, surprise your friend with their favorite candy bar, drop a note in their locker or pick something else you know would make your friend's day.

Art Expression - What makes interactive journaling—interactive is providing different ways to engage with the topic you are working through. Art Expression produces intentional places to express their feelings and unleash their creativity. Provide places to scribble, paint, and color. Black and white coloring pages are popular with teen girls. You can design your own or use already created pintables with permission. Teacherpayteacher. com is a fantastic resource. They have tons of free printables. I've also hired a Fiverr expert to create black and white coloring pages for me.

Power of Words - Our girls are listening to a lot of information out in the world today. *Who* and *what* are they listening to? It's imperative we're able to share the power of words with them. But let's face it, as teenagers, they don't always want to hear what their parents and teachers have to say. This can make it difficult to get these important messages out. Providing purposeful quotes to inspire and empower is effective in sharing messages we want them to internalize. Choose quotes related to your topic or check out music they're listening to and create a quote from a song lyric. Make them coloring pages or blank spaces so they can add a quote. Encourage them to post their quotes in a place they will be seen to serve as a reminder of what they learned; a mirror, door, ceiling, or even their locker at school. For my chapter on friendship, I created a quote from a story I shared in Let's Talk About It. *"Choose kind, inclusive, and encouraging friends, and you will likely be kind, inclusive, and encouraging."* Using a cool font, I made the quote into a black and white poster they could color or doodle on.

Working through insecurities that may trigger mean girl behavior is crucial to cultivating kindness in girl world. Confidence is powerful ammunition against the weapon of insecurity, and interactive journaling is a dynamic tool to help spark confidence and EmbodyKind.

Being a girl and navigating girl world can indeed be tough. I'd love to help you journey through it with a free digital download from my interactive journal *Girl Tough, Identity.* Download the chapter exploring friendships and how they can spark confidence and EmbodyKind. You can find it on The Mean Girl Extinction Project's website; tmgep.com. Just go to the Girl Tough page. Enjoy!

Shaylene King is an author, speaker, and the founder of The Mean Girl Extinction Project, a 501(c)3 non-profit created to address the rise in relational aggression among girls. She teaches girls how to not only survive girl world but to make a difference and thrive in girl world.

Shaylene trains the nation's leading student-led bully prevention program called Safe School Ambassadors. She speaks at schools across the country, equipping students with the tools they need to develop self-confidence and practice and promote a positive social climate on their school campuses.

Shaylene is the author of several books. At the heart of each book is the desire for readers to believe in themselves.

Shaylene lives with her husband in Middle Tennessee, sailing the unchartered waters of empty nesting.

You can find Shaylene and her books at Shayleneking.com

Connect with Shaylene:

Website: https://shayleneking.com

Website: https://tmgep.com

Email: shaylene@shayleneking.com

Instagram: www.instagram.com/shayleneking

Instagram: www.instagram.com/the_mgep

Facebook: www.facebook.com/Shaylenekingbooks

Facebook: www.facebook.com/themeangirlextinctionproject

CHAPTER 4

KINDNESS EQUIVALENT

YOUR PREFERRED LANGUAGE OF KINDNESS

Sarah (SJ) Mackay, MA, Executive Coach

MY STORY

With a few hours of sleep the night prior, I pushed the grocery cart down my local grocery store aisle, quickly skimming across the glossy linoleum floor to get home and get some rest until my weary eyes caught sight of an orange visual delight.

A woman's shopping cart carried nothing except a plant with vibrant orange flowers. Nestled within the medley of flowers, a little white wooden sign spelled "love."

"Those are beautiful," I remarked. The woman had soft eyes, long brown hair, and her face looked tranquil. She asked if I wanted to smell the flowers; I brought my nose to meet the petals and breathed in the faintest whisper of earth.

"This is for my neighbor. She's like my surrogate mother. Well, she stepped in and took care of me," the woman smiled slightly, covering her mouth. She paused and said, "I don't have my top teeth; I'm afraid of the dentist." I nodded with understanding. "People think I was addicted to meth and lost my top teeth, but that's not true. I think people are afraid of me." She held her arm out to show me how far people keep her away.

My heart opened even further, and I could see a kind woman who sought to be known. "I think you're beautiful," I said. She said, "Oh, that's so sweet, let me hug you." Before I could say, "Sure, okay," she had her arms around me. I laughed nervously. We said goodbye amongst the produce and fluorescent lights.

I don't typically hug people at the grocery store. I tend to shop and get out as soon as possible. I've worked my entire life to learn how to navigate anxiety and have successfully found a way to decrease anxiety by finding kindness within to express more kindness outward—my long journey within created new space. The connection and quick hug with the woman left a lasting peaceful impression. Once my car door shut, I began to cry tears of relief and joy. I felt more love in my heart. I hadn't cried in months. It felt good, like warm rain on my face.

The last time I cried was in Africa, stranded at an airport. Exhilarated, I was headed home after a two-week life-changing trip when a man shared the fact that the flight was canceled. This was when I lost any semblance of emotional control. I nodded, pretended to be cool with it, and proceeded to sob in the middle of the open airport. Like any grown adult would do, I collected myself and found a corner. A few dozen of us lay around the waiting room in various bodily contortions—heads on armrests, couples offering a shoulder as a pillow for another, children in the arms of parents, some sitting on the floor. I lay in a ball curled on my coat to avoid the cold cement floor. Knowing I would have plenty of time to ponder what I experienced on my journey, I closed my eyes. I mentally recounted everything I'd seen, heard, smelled, and felt.

I traveled to see a friend who recently moved to Africa. She's the kind of friend who introduces you to new places and encourages you to try something new. Such as when she suggested I take up painting. Oh, and sewing. I had many questions: "Why did you move here? What have you experienced? What has it been like? Who have you become?" She just looked at me sideways quizzically, and then she said flatly, "You ask too many questions." I felt the sting of what she said, my curiosity squashed and tossed out as irrelevant. When I arrived in town, she asked if I would paint a flower for her home. I retreated into her studio to get to work and escape. In the evening, I finished painting and laid the artwork on the coffee table to dry overnight. The next day, in the morning sun, I looked at it with dismay. My friend was in the kitchen making breakfast and wanted to know what I thought of it. I only wanted to know what she thought of it and asked, "What do you think?" She looked at me sideways, frowning. My friend frowns when I play small. "You need to look within," she said with a sigh, hugged me, and walked out of the kitchen.

I can see now she was calling me forward to know the answers lie within—the wisdom runs deep for us all. For my friend, the kindest thing she knew to do for me was to remind me that I had the answers within. Everything I needed was within me. Later that day, she said, "We're going to Kibera to volunteer tomorrow. Would you like to join us?" She said it with that same quizzical look on her face as if to say, "Are you doing okay," and "Let's stop feeling sorry for ourselves."

Just outside Nairobi is Kibera, a slum where 500,000 to one million Africans live and work and a place many children have always called home—almost one square mile of dirt frequently turned to mud from the heavy rainstorms pours on the clusters of tin boxed homes. For a moment, I imagined the rain and wondered what the sound was like on their roofs. A group of us arrived to help serve lunch at the children's community center within the slum. Thick walls divide the school from the rest of the dwellings. My anxiety was at a peak traveling with a group of others, walking into the grounds of the slum, and seeing it for the first time.

Out of fear, I stopped breathing when I first saw the inside of Kibera. Sickness, desperation, and loneliness was my initial perception of the environment.

Two-hundred square foot homes made of tin and mud were configured haphazardly throughout the slum. Each home inhabited anywhere from two to four people with beds and perhaps one table to cook and convene. The main thoroughfare was noticeably uneven, a narrow footpath meandering throughout the slum where all pedestrian traffic moved. Those who inhabited the dwellings walked confidently to and from various buildings.

Outsiders, I imagined, were obvious with their necks craned and peering at their surroundings, including myself. Shops lined the pathways: one shop with basic necessities, some boxed food, small shops with groceries, a used bookstore, and a place to buy t-shirts. Some smiling faces would appear and disappear. Then, a small dirt plot that seemed like it could've been nothing at all grew vegetables to sell. As I walked, I became aware of visiting the spaces in my heart, being with the environment and rock roads; it didn't feel like home, it felt war-torn. Finding acceptance of what existed for so many individuals for so long felt unfathomable, and yet I could see, hear, and feel their reality. I began to judge my surroundings and calculate how many people I could save.

I felt encouraged to do something for someone, buy land, change a life, and make a difference with an act of kindness. Not long after, I met Jennie, a 70-year-old strong, petite woman who moved to Kibera in the 60s. She still lives there today. She wore a t-shirt that said, "Washington," my home state. It felt like a sign to take action. With thoughts of intended kindness, I offered to buy her and the rest of the family a plot of land. As an American, it was a reasonable price. "The land will change her life and generations to come," I told the translator. This was my idea of kindness, and for them, it was an incredible offer also filled with unease and upheaval. Jennie's grandchild stood to inherit a tin home. If Jennie and her family moved, they would have land but no home. The woman's grandson, John, curious and intelligent, ran in and around us as our words were translated back and forth.

Jennie ultimately declined the offer. She told me something I will never forget, "Your kind heart speaks many languages, yet it is not what I need. This is enough for me; I do not need more." I realized with shocking clarity, outside her tin home, that I had assumed my acts of kindness were what she and her entire family needed. If it weren't for her wise soul, I would never have learned this life lesson.

Seven hours after arrival, I realized my first reaction reflected my need for perfection, to not see their suffering, which kept me from truly seeing them and myself. I left Kibera, seeing the surroundings as their home, what they knew, a place of hope, community, and of belonging. The people of Kibera overcame their environment and rose above the tin roofs, mud walls, and timeless struggle to shine as unique, loving humans. Kindness is seeing what's in front of you without judgment, observing others and one's own essence to return to kindness uncluttered with pureness of heart again and again.

Before this trip, I thought kindness only included saving someone, paying for something, or doing something for someone. It meant a world more. It meant being present with someone, connecting and sharing a sense of peace; it's the greatest kindness to give and to receive. It's extraordinary to think that with kindness and compassion, we can bring hope, which I instinctively believe is where we all genuinely meet, no matter where we are from or how we got there. When we see through kind, loving, and unobscured eyes, the invisible becomes the visible. We are faced with our deeper wisdom.

Finding and expressing my kindness historically has required an environment conducive to accessing an open heart. How do I get disengaged from my environment in the first place, I thought? I started to look at my inner life, zoomed in more closely to see where the disconnection occurred, and I realized I didn't know how to authentically express kindness to a person or to myself. I could see that by clearing my ego from my thoughts of kindness, I could return to an authentic way of being.

To see someone for who they are in their environment is to truly witness someone's existence. Not only through our own eyes but through their eyes as well. This is when we can fully observe and learn what might be another's experience and, therefore, the equivalent of kindness.

The inquiry began with the unearthing of my inner voice that demanded I separate myself from others emotionally, physically, and mentally. Throughout my day, and I will admit, my entire life, I've gathered the morsels of microaggressions against myself, which cause disconnection.

Kindness to oneself and others reflects a loving inner life. When I feel my loving nature, it's because I've started connecting, seeing, and feeling what's in and around me. I've equalized my inner world with my outer world and found my kindness equivalent, showing the expression of the love within.

Is it possible I'm having a breakthrough in kindness at a grocery store parking lot? No, I told myself that would be too easy and too convenient. Yet, I checked in with my heart and wisdom and knew the experiences in

Africa, and the woman in the grocery store somehow created an equivalent for me, a formula for kindness.

I started my car, breathed deeply, and drove home a little slower, more aware of my surroundings and the peaceful humming in my head. Once home, I began drafting the letter to Jennie in Africa. I didn't know how I'd get her the letter or how I would see her again—the woman who wisely told me to sing my song of kindness and to listen for the equivalent of the other person's song. Her wisdom, her breathtaking beautiful soul, and a woman at home within herself—her equivalent of kindness is to offer peace to another and recognize the universal language of kindness.

Seeking the equivalent of kindness in relation to others helps one gain clarity and discover self-compassion within, so you may express it outward. To truly feel the connection kindness brings, we need to find the kindness equivalent for others. What does the other person need?

Meditation will allow one to expand and make room for kindness in our heart. One will be able to have more freedom to express the equivalent of loving-kindness that's within and express it outwards by letting go of unneeded perceptions.

"This is not mine; this am I not, this is not myself."

~Samyutta Nikaya

THE PRACTICE

Begin by noticing your breath.
Allow the breath to flow inward and outward.
Be with the rhythm.
Breathing in.
Breathing out.
Each breath in releases you to fully embrace the present.
And each breath out releases emotions and thoughts that don't serve you.
Breathe in, fresh new air.

Breathe out and release.

Breathe in.

Breathe out.

Pause.

Welcome to the present moment. Before we begin, remind yourself that this time is for you. Allow no distractions, no worries, and no to-do lists to interfere with your time.

Take a moment to make yourself comfortable where you are. Maybe straighten your back or trace gentle circles with the nose, relaxing your neck. Once you've reached a place of stillness, begin to deepen your breath. In through the nose and out through the mouth. Again.

Turn your awareness to the ground beneath you. Firm. Strong. As you continue to breathe, travel from the crown of the head down. Feel the crown grow light like a feather, and then carry on down.

The forehead.

The mouth.

Feel the ribcage loosen and float upwards. As you breathe, it becomes harder and harder to keep yourself anchored to the ground as your freed upper body pulls you upwards. Resist it as you travel on down through the arms and belly. When you reach your hips, visualize releasing further on the count of three.

One. Two. Three.

Go through the rest of your body and gently release it. Thighs. Knees. All the way down to the feet. Mental countdown from the big toe to the pinky. One. Two. Three. Four. Feel that pinky loosen and let go. Five. You are free.

Exercise link: http://mackaycoaching.com/meditations

I work with individuals to support them in gaining clarity by accessing their inner wisdom. We do this by developing a clearer and deeper understanding of their feelings and their actions for more kindness towards oneself and others.

Sarah is a senior trainer for licensed sponsors of Dale Carnegie Training. She works closely with Dale Carnegie business consultants and their clients to design and deliver customized programs and workshops to address their specific objectives. Sarah has worked with numerous Fortune 500 companies, technology, finance, mortgage, and agricultural machinery industries to help them strengthen their abilities to reduce employee turnover, operate with confidence, enhance people skills, strengthen communication skills, and improve upon diversity and inclusion.

Education and Certifications: Master's degree in Leadership and Communication from Gonzaga University. Master's degree in Counseling from Northwestern University. BA in Journalism and Public Relations, Dale Carnegie Course Facilitator, Design Your Life Coach, Accomplishment Coaching (ICF certified), 200-hour Yoga Alliance Certified, and meditation instructor training.

Connect with Sarah:

LinkedIn: https: //www.linkedin.com/in/mackaysarahcoaching/

Instagram: congruentdesigncoaching

CHAPTER 5

SELF-FORGIVENESS

FROM PAIN TO PEACE

Karlie Everhart, MA

MY STORY

I never thought I'd find myself here, in prison, yet there I was, 32 years old, sitting in a cold gymnasium.

The walls had rich stories to tell, ones I'd be eager to hear but know I never would. The gym was hard and gray—much like the hearts of the people that fill this place—at least that's what society thinks. Yet I felt very different. There was part of me that felt safe there. Outside, the sun was shining, but inside it was quite chilly and smelled like a sterile dental office. I was sitting in a chair, excited and nervous. I was wearing black jeans and my husband's black cashmere sweater. I could feel the chill of the floor through my black converse sneakers. I was one of few women in a sea of men.

My eyes shifted nervously around the room as inmates shuffled in. I took turns staring at the cement floor my feet were planted on and at the inmates finding their seats beside me. I'd make eye contact just long enough to say *I see you* and for them to confirm, *You're safe here.* I'd flash a half-smile, and my eyes would shift back to the cement floor. I see you.

You're safe here—cement floor. I see you. *You're safe* here—cement floor. This happened for the next 15 minutes until we all settled in.

Although prison was a place I had been at least a dozen times over the last three years, all with Freedom to Choose, this time felt different. Freedom to Choose was an organization I volunteered with whose mission is to "transform the lives of individuals impacted by incarceration through compassionate experiential education." We were at the men's Substance Abuse Treatment Facility and State Prison (SATF) in Corcoran, California, teaching the inmates about identifying emotional triggers, releasing judgments, and positive self-talk.

The two-day workshop consisted of five trios. In each trio, we taught a new skill. Inmates left the workshop with a total of five skills. A trio is a format of sharing that involves three people: a client, a facilitator, and an observer. Each person gets 20 minutes in every position. A bell rings, indicating the start and end times. Upon the second bell ringing, everyone rotates to the next position. To build trust, the volunteers always start as the client. It's a way to model to the inmates that it's safe to be vulnerable, as most have never learned this way of communication. This time I started as the client and was being facilitated by an inmate. I'll call him Paul.

Paul was in his mid-50s, with salt and pepper hair and tan skin. If he was in the free world, he looked as though he'd smell like a tanning bed and Axe deodorizing spray. He had a full sleeve of tattoos on both arms that looked like they'd been inked in his 20s. He revealed to me that he was serving a life sentence—we didn't get into what his crime was. It didn't matter to me as I also felt like I was serving a life sentence, one of intense self-criticism. His appearance was hard, but his energy was warm—what I imagine my father to be like.

Previously, I participated in these workshops at the women's facilities. This time I deliberately volunteered at SATF out of a desire to know my father. He spent the better half of his 50-plus years behind bars, mostly due to his drug addiction. While he wasn't at this particular facility, I tried to better understand myself by connecting with my father's experience.

Very few people knew about my biological father; I hardly knew him. It was easy keeping this close to the chest as my mother built us a wonderful life with another man, my dad. I've never met my biological father and have only spoken to him a handful of times. The biggest impact he had on my life was that he wasn't there. From as young as I can remember, I told myself I wasn't good enough because he chose drugs over being present in my life. This set me on a path of extreme mental and emotional anguish, bankrupt of self-acceptance, and an insatiable curiosity to know myself.

This face-to-face meeting with a stranger, who could be my dad but wasn't, was an opportunity to get some answers. Why was I not enough for my father to stick around? Who would I be if he had? Little did I know that Paul would grant me the insight that would reframe years of pain and self-work I'd already done.

Life, B.P. *(before Paul)* was very different. From an outsider looking in, things looked perfect.

I was tall, thin, and had the right clothes, the girl next door. I was approachable, dependable, and familiar. I was a prom princess and a pageant queen. I thrived in social affairs and academic affairs. I played soccer, softball, and volleyball and was a cheerleader. I volunteered in retirement homes and spoke to young kids about the adverse effects of using drugs. I checked all the boxes. Life was good—at least that's what I wanted you to believe.

On the inside, life was very different than it seemed.

I had a lot of friends but always felt alone. I shared just enough of myself for people to wave at me in the halls but not to call on the weekend. I was likable but never felt like I belonged. A lot of the time, I was too scared to ask my "friends" if I could sit with them at lunch, so I would get my food and then slowly walk past the lunch tables to secure a last-minute invitation. Some days I received one. On other days I would find a place to sit alone, in the back of the building, where nobody could see me. Sitting alone felt far less painful than asking and being told "no."

It was the summer going into my sophomore year of high school that my disordered eating began. I gained 25 pounds that summer. To me, that weight was heavier than what the scale indicated. It solidified that I wasn't enough. I made those extra pounds mean I was unlovable, that nobody would want to be friends with me, and that I would be alone forever.

To numb the pain, I would binge eat. In public, I'd mostly eat salads, but in the privacy of my own pain, when everyone in my house was asleep, I would sneak downstairs. I made heaping plates of whatever was in the refrigerator, brought them back to my bedroom, and ate them in the dark, along with the candy hidden in the drawers beside my bed. I ate until I felt like I would burst, and then I followed it up with a steady helping of shame and judgment or a trip to the bathroom to throw it all up.

In an attempt to lose weight, I popped Ex-Lax pills. They had a blue, sugary coating and a sweet smell, and if you left them in your hand for too long, they'd stain your hands blue, just like the candy I hid in my drawers. I developed a tolerance quite quickly, so at one point, I was eating 15-20 pills a day. Taking laxatives was less invasive and easier to hide than throwing up.

It was in college when I finally mustered up the courage to seek help for the first time. I went to an Overeaters Anonymous meeting. I sat through the mostly-boring meeting and afterward was interested in talking with the attendees, hoping they would set me on a path to freedom. What ended up happening was quite the opposite. I was too thin to be taken seriously as an overeater and too big to relate with the people experiencing anorexia and bulimia, so I was ignored and discarded, just as my father did.

Over the next few years, I settled into a career in advertising. By the time I was 29 years old, I had overseen a team of 17 people. I had a fancy job title to go along with my fancy salary, a cute boyfriend, and loads of friends. I thought I'd finally be happy once I had all these things. I'd prove to myself, my family, and the world that I was enough, I was lovable, and I belonged. Most of those things just left me unhappy and lonelier than I had ever been. Something had to change.

I had heard about the University of Santa Monica (USM) from my best friend's mother. She attended, and it completely transformed her life, so I decided I would attend.

During the three intense years I was studying at USM, I spent 900 hours in the classroom, learned over 50 principles and practices that are the foundation of my coaching practice today, healed many deep wounds, and learned how to be kind to myself. It was hard and painful, but I was committed.

It was also the first time I learned what self-forgiveness was. The format of our school weekends was spent in a trio, the same format used in Freedom to Choose. The one consistent thing about all the trios was that they all ended with self-forgiveness. I learned that to forgive yourself is to accept yourself. I spent hundreds of hours forgiving myself, which solidified that self-acceptance is the greatest act of kindness.

In the beginning, it felt silly to me. How could I forgive myself if I still judged myself? I was encouraged to keep going. Chop wood, carry water. So I did. Over time something started to happen. Like peeling back the layers of an onion, I began shedding decades of stories I made up about myself. I started to let go of the beliefs that I didn't belong, that I wasn't worthy, and that I wasn't loveable. I started to believe that I was perfect, exactly the way that I am. I *am* worthy. *I do* belong. *I am* lovable.

Three-quarters of the way through school, I noticed my life was changing in extraordinary ways. I practiced self-forgiveness multiple times a day. Whenever I caught myself judging or speaking negatively about myself, I would forgive. I had fully bought into what my teachers told me, that self-forgiveness is the pathway to freedom. I embodied kindness, love, and self-acceptance, and it had a huge impact and not just in the way I treated myself. Things on the outside also changed. I nearly tripled my salary, was promoted at work, and had deeper and more fulfilling conversations with friends because I shared more of myself with them. My boyfriend became my fiance. I found my voice and prioritized my needs. I was feeling so much more confident in who I was. I knew that my existence mattered and that I was important.

Although I did a lot of work, the feelings of unworthiness still lingered. I knew I had more work to do, so I traded in my school books for a weekend in prison. There I was, an affluent girl from Orange County, California, behind bars, guilty for living a life riddled with shame, blame, and judgment carrying my father's absence like an annoying cold you can't shake.

The workshop was about to start. My nerves built like the pressure in a volcano as I sat facing Paul. The chairs are packed in so tightly our knees are practically touching. The bell rang, indicating it was time to begin. "My father was a drug addict. I've never met him. His absence always made me feel like I wasn't enough." Paul listens intently as I speak, "But why couldn't he get his act together? He's so selfish. I've spent my whole life trying to figure out what's wrong with me. Contemplating what I could've done to make things different." As I speak, I'm surprised at the weight my story still carries after working on these same issues for years already. I forgave myself and continued. Paul listened. Nodding to confirm he understood, perhaps part of him felt the same. He stayed with me the entire time as if to be holding my hand and walking the path with me.

I continue pouring my heart out to him. I feel safe with him. "There *must* be something wrong with me because *if* I were enough, my Dad would have gotten sober years ago," I say. Paul stops me. He took a deep breath and began to speak, "What if you were *so* important that knowing you exist has kept him alive all these years?" This comment is when everything clicked for me. It was an invitation to be kind to myself. My father's absence wasn't the issue; the real issue is what I made it all mean. I didn't need to forgive my father. I needed to forgive myself for making his absence mean I wasn't enough. The truth is I was more than enough, and his absence had absolutely no impact on my enoughness.

The euphoria of forgiving myself so deeply warmed me from the inside out, like drinking a hot chocolate on a cold winter's day. So there I sat, behind bars, tears streaming down my face, a free woman for the very first time.

THE PRACTICE

PURPOSE/BENEFITS:

To experience inner peace, lightness, and positivity.

To experience loving-kindness toward yourself and others.

To let go of beliefs that are no longer serving you so that you can live a life that lights you up.

To free yourself from any judgment, misidentifications, or misbeliefs that you might be carrying around.

To allow yourself to connect to the truth of who you are—a soul who is having a human experience.

Using the tool: Compassionate Self-Forgiveness can be used whenever you judge yourself or others or buy into beliefs about yourself and others that you're ready to let go of. It can be used on smaller issues like judging someone you pass on the street or on larger issues like shame, a boss yelling at you, or an argument with a partner, child, or friend.

The first few times you practice Compassionate Self-Forgiveness, you might not believe the forgiveness or truth. It's okay to fake it until you make it. Over time, if you stick with it, the judgments will fall away, and you will experience inner peace.

PRACTICING COMPASSIONATE SELF-FORGIVENESS

1. Take a moment to set a clear and positive intention. (Note: the first few times you practice Compassionate Self-Forgiveness, you may want to find a quiet place. Over time you'll be able to practice forgiveness wherever you are.)

2. Connect with your high power.

3. Think of a time when you were upset. What was going on? What were you feeling? What were you experiencing in your body?

4. Now ride that feeling all the way back to the very first time you can remember experiencing it. How old were you? What was going on at that moment? Who was there? Bring that moment to life. Feel into it.

5. What was so upsetting or objectionable for you at that moment?

6. What were the stories you made up about who you are or who they are?

7. Make a list of all the judgments, misbeliefs, or misidentifications you created at that time. For example: I'm not enough. He was a jerk. If I was enough, he would've gotten sober. I am a burden. He was weak.

8. Forgive yourself for the judgments, misbeliefs, or misidentifications you identified above by following any of the scripts below. Continue until you've forgiven all the judgments you identified.

    a. "I forgive myself for judging myself as. . ."

        i. Example: I forgive myself for judging myself as not being good enough.

    b. "I forgive myself for judging others as. . ."

      i. Example: I forgive myself for judging my father as being weak.

    c. "I forgive myself for buying into the belief that. . ."

      i. Example: "I forgive myself for buying into the belief that if I was enough, my father would have gotten sober."

9. State what the truth is for each judgment, misbelief, or misidentification you just forgave:

    a. The truth is:

      i. I am enough.

      ii. My father has always been doing the best that he can.

      iii. My enoughness has nothing to do with my father's sobriety.

      iv. I am worthy because I exist.

10. Take a deep breath and connect with the loving essence that is your essential nature.

Karlie Everhart, MA, graduated from Loyola Marymount University in 2009 with a Bachelor's degree in International Business and Entrepreneurship and a minor in Art History. She spent seven years working in the advertising industry for companies such as Mindshare, Evolve Media, and Clique Media. She spent the better half of her corporate career in leadership roles. At one point, she was responsible for guiding and mentoring a team of 17.

After graduating from the University of Santa Monica in 2016 with a Master's degree in Spiritual Psychology and an emphasis on Consciousness, Health, and Healing, she opened her practice as a life and career coach. She is committed to supporting people who wish to experience their own authentic empowerment.

When Karlie's not speaking at events, supporting her one-on-one and group coaching clients, or hosting corporate workshops, you can find her volunteering with Freedom to Choose and A Place Called Home. She also enjoys writing her bi-weekly blog, spending time outdoors, traveling the world, and practicing transcendental meditation. She currently resides in Los Angeles with her family.

Connect with Karlie:

Website: https://www.karlieeverhart.com/

Email: karlie@karlieeverhart.com

Instagram: www.instagram.com/karlieeverhart

Facebook: https://www.facebook.com/KarlieEverhartCoaching/

LinkedIn: https://www.linkedin.com/in/karlie-everhart/

CHAPTER 6

UNITY THROUGH CREATIVITY

POWERING THE SINGING TREE MURAL PROJECT

Laurie Marshall, MA, Spiritual Art Activist for Peace

MY STORY

And a Child Shall Lead Them

In 1999, after I painted a 24' x 4' mural with all 130 students at Hillsboro Elementary School in rural Virginia, eight-year-old Meredith Miller said, "I wish the whole world could see our painting, and then the whole world would be happy." Then she asked, "What if the whole world made a painting together?"

Bam! My soul's longing for peace, harmony, and unity was met in this vision. What an impossible task—to invite the whole world to create together! If all of humanity could consciously work together on a painting, it would demonstrate how we can work together to make a peaceful world.

"Who am I to do this?" My coach, Karen Bading, said, "Who are you not to?" "How am I to do this?" I didn't have a clue. The model of trees and forests springs to mind as a structure for a series of murals. I attended a conflict resolution conference with my father in San Sebastian, Spain, when a young teacher from Ireland was puzzling about how she could bring the Catholic and Protestant children together. I suggested making a painting of a tree, with children from both sides making leaves. The very subject I gave up drawing as a child, which you will hear about later, became the key to my life's work.

The universe also reinforced the importance of trees in the "how" of inviting the whole world to make a painting together. Someone handed me Kate Seredy's book *The Singing Tree.* She tells the story of her father, who was a soldier in World War I:

> One night, my battalion crawled all night long on our bellies to escape the enemy. Everything had been destroyed by war. When the dawn came, one tree was still alive. Birds from hundreds of miles away, who aren't normally together, filled the tree, singing a song that had never been heard before.

I see the Earth as the Singing Tree of the solar system. All the things that divide us are not as important as the fact that we are unified in life on Earth, floating in space. We can choose to destroy each other and our Earth or create something beautiful, like the new song of the birds in *The Singing Tree.* We can choose to generate unity through creativity—not through coercion, bombs, and bullets.

In 2002, I founded the Unity Through Creativity Foundation to use the arts as a peace-building tool, with the goal of transforming pain into purpose, trauma into beauty, and division into connection.

What is the Singing Tree Mural Process?

- It's a way to be a part of the whole world creating together.
- It's making a mural with people to envision a positive future and spark innovation using the model of trees and forests.
- It's honoring that the Creator is in all of us and that we each have a unique contribution to add to the miracle of life in the universe.
- It's a practice combining peace literacy, communication skills, and visual art.

- It's an intergenerational, mycelial network of people who are upping the positive vibration of the planet.
- It's a way to have heart-centered conversations where every voice and vision matter and new ideas rise up.
- It's a way to be creative in the community and celebrate with painting, art, song, dancing, and storytelling.
- It's unity through creativity—not through force.

The Singing Tree Mural Project embodies kindness.

How did I get here?

On a winding and circuitous route, beginning with:

THE QUAKER PARADOX

My parents were both only children and didn't have much understanding of the competitive dynamics of three young daughters. Our mom was raised Lutheran in a central Pennsylvania rural culture, and our dad was raised as a secular Jew in New York City. They met at Bucknell University during World War II. Seeking a religion that made sense to both of them, they chose Quakerism. They resonated with the non-hierarchical Quaker belief that everyone has a Divine light within them, the silent meetings for worship to listen for guidance from Creator, and the emphasis on good deeds in the world.

At nine years old in 1958, I went to a Quaker conference in Cape May, New Jersey, with my family. Inside a long narrow hall, I felt the resonance of an electric voice that filled the crowded, creaky building. Waves of the Atlantic Ocean crashed below us. I couldn't see the man who was speaking. I only saw the grown-up's waists and shoulders. I experienced a contagious excitement. The man's voice was a deep song. I remember his words, "People of all colors can live together like sisters and brothers." The man was Martin Luther King, Jr. My soul was imprinted with this message.

Slap! My childhood was disrupted by a crack in the strongly held values of my parents. Slap! That was the sound of my father hitting my sister across the face. Slap! That was the sound of the pot-stick breaking on her backside. I don't hear her cry. My parents, Alice and Stan Marshall were able to meet most of the needs of their oldest and youngest children, but not my middle sister. She was not a traditional learner, which teachers and our parents did not understand. My parents didn't handle her frustration and anger well, sometimes using physical violence against her. "After you slap her, she's good for a couple of months," my father would say.

I felt paralyzed by a terrible quandary. Quakers strive for non-violence, yet my parents justified violence against my sister. I didn't stop the violence, and I didn't speak up against it. I froze and felt guilty, helpless, and numb.

So, as a child, I learned there could be a gap between who people want to be and who they are. I witnessed the challenge of having the unity of one's inner experience, the values expressed, and the actions taken resulting in conflict. As an adult, I see that challenge in myself to this day. Getting closer to the joyous peace-builder I want to be has required lifelong self-reflection, constant learning from mentors—who include children, openness to feedback about my blind spots, and expressing myself creatively.

TREES

I am ten. I draw trees. My family goes on camping trips every summer, where we are all together—a rare treat with my father's long work hours and my out-of-reach sisters in higher grades at school. I feel happy and excited on these adventures close to the Earth, the stars, and the mountains. On these camping trips and our suburban streets, trees capture my imagination. I find their smells, textures, grace, changes, variety, and roots reaching down and branches reaching up endlessly fascinating—that they house birds, which I also love, adds to their mesmerizing hold. I feel unified with the trees and the life they support. To express my love, I set out to draw tree after tree with their millions of leaves. I try to draw each leaf. I am overwhelmed, daunted, and frustrated. After many weeks of failure, I give up—not only drawing trees but drawing altogether. My confidence dashed. No one told me I could draw the big simple shape of the tree. Getting lost in the details prevents me from seeing the whole. I stop making any effort to capture what I see and express what I love.

FINDING THE POWER OF CREATOR THROUGH HEARTBREAK AND CREATIVITY

As an extreme extrovert, I do not have easy access to my inner experience. During my childhood, I was often in a state of frozen numbness. It took me until I was in my 30s to realize that I could have two feelings, like anger and love, at once—something many ten-year-olds realize.

Marrying my college teacher at the age of 20 and divorcing him at the age of 23 did not fit into the story I created about my future. When we split up, I dislocated my knee, and he dislocated his shoulder in the same week. Despite the profound pain, I was left with two gifts from the failed marriage. Divorce cracked the ice around my heart, and I rediscovered drawing. My ex-husband believed that everyone is an artist and supported drawing and painting as part of daily life. When I drew, images appeared on the paper as if from an unknown source. Despair, sadness, anger, frustration, fear, and terror showed up. As the pictures appear, the unconscious hold of the feelings dwindles. My inner light also shows up, giving me a sense of being unified with the Creator. I see that I had an endless abundance of ideas within me. I'm less afraid and more generous. I'm kinder. What an amazing and accessible process.

Because I wanted to share the healing power of art in all my enthusiastic extroversion, I went on to get a Master's Degree in Community Arts from Beacon College in 1980, combining my love of being with people and sharing the tool of art to express, heal and connect. There was no such field at that time, so the official transcripts say Art and Education. Since that time, I have devoted my life to supporting young people and adults in understanding their gifts, talents, and purpose using Project-Based Learning and Arts Integration. I move in and out of being a classroom teacher and being an artist-in-residence in Virginia, Pennsylvania, and California. The first Singing Tree Mural began in 2001 with 1,000 students from Rappahannock County, Virginia's public school, private school, and homeschool communities.

THE MAGICAL PROCESS

And so, in over 20 years, the Singing Tree Mural process has emerged to help any family, community, organization, business, or city envision a positive future and spark innovation. The painting process is based on nature's diversity, clear goals, lack of micro-management, abundance, replicability, endless creativity, interconnectedness, and generosity. The structure of each mural begins with a tree on the Earth in space. At this writing, 107 murals have been made by over 21,000 people from 52 countries.

Beginning with a heartbreak or community challenge, intergenerational design teams have addressed such issues as freedom from addiction, autism, restorative justice, healing the trauma of war, climate solutions, transforming political and religious division, the gift of femininity, grief, supplanting violence with peace, gratitude, and kindness.

There's a story about negotiations that had been stalled between Palestinians. Then one day, someone's truck broke down. Both parties went out and fixed the truck. When they came back, they could finally reach an agreement. The Singing Tree Mural Project is the broken-down truck that lets alienated and conflicting parties see that collaboration is possible. When we create, the Creator shows up. We can talk with each other more easily when we have a common small goal.

One student said, after making *The Singing Tree of Climate Solutions* in Ukiah, California, "If we can make this amazing mural in 12 days, it gives me hope we can turn around climate change." When a member of the Crips gang in Pittsburgh, Pennsylvania, saw the artwork made by a Blood gang member, he said, "Man, I didn't know he had that in him." A Republican expressed surprise when her artwork was appreciated by numerous Democrats in *The Singing Tree of What Makes America Great.* "All fighting stopped when we worked on the mural because we knew we were part of something bigger," reported a middle school student in San Francisco.

The Singing Tree Mural process involves making shared agreements, meeting in a circle, peace literacy training, understanding the neurobiology of communication, and learning skills in conflict resolution, restorative practices, and artmaking. When the painting is complete, there is a multi-media celebration, planning for the next step, and the planting of the tree(s) that are honored in the mural.

Since I established the Singing Tree Mural Certification, people around the world are learning to facilitate Singing Tree Murals in their communities. Unity Through Creativity has also begun the **5 x 5 Mural Program**–five Singing Tree murals over five years. **5 x 5's** have begun in Cyprus, England, Uganda, Mozambique, Peru, and the United States.

As we face mass migrations, climate disasters, pandemics, and unforeseen challenges, we need to practice envisioning, collaborating, and creating ingenious solutions. I believe we can call upon the Creator within us and connect to the Creator within others to honor the Earth we have been blessed with. I believe we can thrive in this unprecedented and traumatic time. Over and over, I see the collective beauty and genius in people. The Singing Tree Mural Project is one way to demonstrate and embody kindness—a doable short-term goal to give us hope. If you long for unity, peace, and kindness, I invite you to add to your voice and vision to the growing forest of Singing Tree murals. Create a mural in your community. Add to a mural that is the works. Get certified to bring peace-building through art—inspired by nature. We are all in this together. The whole world is invited!

THE PRACTICE

THE SINGING TREE MURAL PRACTICE

Below you'll find the first steps for a three-to-five person collaborative painting outlined in a 1.5-hour session. Two more sessions and a more detailed materials list are available at www.unitythroughcreativity.org/free-offer. No art experience is needed. Trust that, just as your iris is unique, your thumbprint is unique, and your DNA is unique—you have unique and powerful images the world needs to see. Humans have been drawing for over 60,000 years. We've been writing for 5,000. Trust your hand.

Materials:

A large piece of paper
Computer paper to draw leaves, birds, stars, etc.
Colored pencils
Watercolors
Paintbrushes
Glue sticks
Scissors
Manilla folder

STEP 1 OF 3 TO CREATE A SINGING TREE WITH THREE-TO-FIVE PEOPLE

Session 1 – 1.5 hours

1. Make agreements about how you have the most fun doing a project together (examples):

    a. Put-ups, not put-downs of self and others

    b. All ideas welcome

    c. Be kind

    d. Mistakes are useful opportunities

2. Decide if you'll make decisions by consensus or majority.

3. Read *The Singing Tree* story, and the paragraph included above. The structure of *The Singing Tree* is a tree on the Earth in space.

4. Make a decision about what challenge you want to envision a positive future for, what heartbreak, and what concern. This subject is the theme of your Singing Tree. It can be personal. It can be about your community. It can be about the world.

5. Turn the challenge into its solution. Example: *The Singing Tree of Freedom from Addiction, The Ukrainian Singing Tree of Strength and Freedom, The Singing Tree of Kindness, The Singing Tree to Prevent Extinction.*

6. Chose a native tree to honor.

7. Decide if you want to make the painting horizontal or vertical.

8. Each person makes their own drawing in a horizontal or vertical box, coloring in all the white space. Decide how you want to portray the Earth and the universe: Include planets, moons, nebulae, or whatever you want in the galaxy.

9. Look at all the drawings and combine different elements from each drawing into one drawing—the Master Design. Be sure all the white space is filled.

10. Make the galaxy by taping the watercolor paper around the edges of a board. Wet the whole paper with your three-inch brush. Add the colors of the galaxy. Spatter the universe with white paint for stars. Let the painting dry. Give it another spray of stars.

Go to https://www.unitythroughcreativity.org/embody-kind-free-gift for Steps 2 and 3. Enjoy!

For 40 years, Author, Innovator, and Artist **Laurie Marshall** has empowered youth and adults through creative collaboration. She practices Peace Building through Art, inspired by nature. A visionary educator, she has served mostly low-income children, families, and their schools as an Arts Integration and Project-Based Learning Specialist. Her mission is to nurture creativity, a love of learning, and a collaborative spirit. She is the founder of the Unity Through Creativity Foundation and the Singing Tree Project.

In addition, Laurie is at certified K-12 art and social studies teacher with training in the Waldorf Curriculum, Conversational Intelligence, Peace Literacy, and Outward Bound. Her MA in art and education from Beacon College laid the groundwork for her innovative use of visual art and storytelling in consensus building, leadership training, and conflict prevention. Clients have included NASA, FEMA, the Army Corps of Engineers, the Department of Interior, the US Botanical Gardens, as well as public schools, hospitals, and prisons around the United States. After 15 years in California, she now lives in El Paso, Texas, with her husband to be close to her grandchildren. She is a fierce elder—passionate in her dedication to the well-being of families and all the grandchildren, those who care for them, and the remarkable planet that supports life in the solar system.

Connect with Laurie:

Laurie@UnityThroughCreativity.org

https://www.unitythroughcreativity.org/

https://www.unitythroughcreativity.org/the-singing-tree-project

https://www.unitythroughcreativity.org/singing-tree-certification

CHAPTER 7

PARENTING WITH PURPOSE

HELPING KIDS SPEAK UP WITH CONFIDENCE

Kristin Ray, Author, Speaker

MY STORY

This morning started like many before it and many that would come after—with the heart-pounding jolt of an iPhone alarm. Energy rushed through my body as I desperately pounded the tousled sheets around me, searching for the blaring culprit. After the panic of finding that red stop button on my iPhone subsided, I remembered something amazing that had been a part of my life for the last few weeks; *oh yeah, I'm pregnant.*

My body ached with the exhaustion of a second-trimester mother, but my heart fluttered with excitement. It had been about two weeks now since we'd been to the doctor to make sure everything with the pregnancy was in order. I'd even been able to take a blood test which, among other things, would tell us the gender of this precious life we were waiting on.

The waiting felt torturous. On the way to work that morning, my mind spun with bright possibilities for names, nursery themes, and baby shower games. I'm a planner and, by nature, planners are control freaks. So, naturally, biding my time before that anticipated results call was specifically formidable for my personality. On this day, though, I was so busy at work the sound of the ringer on my phone almost went ignored in the chaos of the office. As I looked down at my phone, probably on the last ring before it went to voicemail, I saw the caller ID, and it read: Doctor. Time came to a sudden halt, now passing in ultra-slow motion, as I slid my frantic finger across the phone to answer it. I could only faintly hear the nurse's echoey words as she said, "The baby is healthy." Her next words, however, I heard with stunning clarity. "Do you want to know the gender?"

What kind of asinine question was that, I thought, as my breathing started to pick up. *Wait! I want to experience this amazing, life-altering thing with the man I love.* So, I uncharacteristically decided to be patient.

"Would you mind sharing this news with a friend so I can be surprised with my husband?" I asked the nurse, barely believing this skilled display of personal patience.

And just like that, the only human in the world who knew the gender of my baby became two. My friend lovingly typed up the results and placed them in an envelope that might as well have been a vault. Somehow, I resisted the urge to rip it open and regain the control I felt I was lacking in this seemingly endless unknown while I walked to lunch, where I was meeting my husband. It was one of those days that couldn't have been more beautiful. The sun warmed my face perfectly without inducing a drop of sweat. As I slid on my rose-gold aviators, I breathed in the fresh air and reminded myself with glee that I was pregnant—this cherished state that I so longed to be in, and we were about to find out the gender. I don't know why we felt there was so much mystery.

We're obviously having a boy, I casually reassured myself. For some reason, we'd never considered our baby might be a girl. We both had always wanted a boy. My husband and I were perfectly aligned on that.

As I eagerly met my husband's glance from across the cafeteria parking lot, my feet skipped over to him as I couldn't hold back my excitement any longer. We took the stairs up to the cafeteria two at a time, which left me even more breathless than normal, as I was both out-of-shape and pregnant. We chose one of the largest booths in the place. It could have held ten average-sized humans. I'm guessing we felt this was the best booth for us because the presence of this amazing secret felt like it took up a lot of room. My eyes locked with those of my nervous husband as I sat the envelope on the expansive, empty table in front of us. Our hearts hammered, his with the apprehension of a new father, mine with delight and anticipation.

So, there we were, vault in hand, deciding to unlock this life-changing information and breathe it out into the world. I carefully tore open the envelope so as not to render it unsaveable; after all, this was a keep-sake moment. And then, all the heart-pounding jubilation crashed down. The letter read: "It's a girl." I had no words for the feelings that flooded my body and mind. I slumped over into my husband's arms. Outwardly, I was silent and still—a rare speechless moment. Inside, complete panic.

No, no, wait, this can't be right! I can't have a girl—I'm too broken. The universe has to know that I can't handle this, right?

Next, the tears came. Not like subtle raindrops or the flow of a river, but like a dam. The maximum number of tears that my lower lids would hold just sat there, ready to spill over, as I begged them not to do so in this very public space.

Just about a year before this pivotal day, once vague and blurry memories of childhood sexual abuse came screaming back into my mind with crystal clarity. With these memories came the realization I was not who I had always seen myself as. I was still awash in my victimhood. I had just recently come to terms with being a statistic, and "Survivor" was not yet a title I was able to embrace. It had taken all the pick-myself-up attitude I could muster in the months since to get through a wedding, a new marriage, and the beginning of this pregnancy with any sense of normalcy and strength. It was a day-to-day battle to keep my head above the waves of sadness that came with slowly mourning my childhood. Surely, I could not be expected now to birth a little girl and begin the art of somehow protecting her from a fate similar to the one my childhood was met with.

Next came the anger.

Seriously, this too? This trauma is going to permeate into this moment, too? I anguished, just trying not to give up.

Then the exhaustion from the morning returned. I couldn't fathom how I could take on the mental commitment this venture would require of me, in addition to the just-staying-upright I'd been attempting for around a year. Then, I met my husband's eyes.

"It's going to be okay," he said, just slightly less confidently than we both needed him to.

This was something he'd said to me so many times over the past few months that I'm sure we both lost count. Like normal, he put his own tumultuous experience aside for a moment (he was panicking in his own mind about all the things that might challenge a normal father of a daughter) to get me through the trepidation I was feeling.

Then something changed in me. Just as quickly as the dread of this news arrived, it dissolved. I was overcome with a brand-new feeling that calmed the hurricane brewing inside. I had the sensation that my mind and my heart suddenly decided to sit up straight. My soul breathed in, and I dug up a resolve I didn't know I had in the depths of my being. Now, years later, having felt this way many more times, I can identify what came over me so suddenly. This was my first experience with feeling the instinct of a mother—the sensation a mother gets when she is undoubtedly willing to walk to the ends of the earth to protect her child. This fear of being too broken to be my daughter's mother was the first thing that threatened her, and I decided to attack it with the ferocity only a mother knows. It is with that ferocity I accepted her and the challenges that were to come for us. Absorbed with fear and focus, I turned my attention to my duties as her mother. This day was another that I had to survive and then choose to make something of. That something I made that day was a plan.

Looking back, that day sticks with me because of the extreme ups and downs the three of us experienced together. Even now, with a four-year-old, we experience similar extremes as I parent through my trauma. For our family, this means emotion-filled moments when triggers arise, usually as a result of tasks that look and feel too unbearably similar to a childhood stolen away. The one thing that seems to even out the fluctuation of my feelings is remembering I made a plan that day. That plan unknowingly became what I now call the Four M's—a process by which I hold myself accountable for preparing her for all that her life may throw at her. The plan brings control and structure to the deluge of fear that comes with being a stunted girl and mothering a girl of my own. I plan to raise a stronger, more aware, more self-assured girl than I was. I will intentionally and with purpose provide her with the necessary skills to use her voice, trust her instincts and mind, and speak her truth in ways I was unable to as a child. This is the kindness I attempt to embody every day in my home and out in our world.

THE PRACTICE

The practice of the Four M's provides a roadmap for parents who want to teach their children the power of their voice. As a set of four, these tactics will guide you through intentionally teaching the young people you care for the basics of being fearless. The Four M's consist of: Mark, Model, Message, and Motivate.

MARK

For our purposes, Mark is defined as: to label or identify. To shape kids who are brave enough to take on their fears in a meaningful way, they first have to understand which fears serve a positive purpose and which are disadvantageous. When we practice marking, we help our kids identify specifically which fears are keeping them safe or, in contrast, are keeping them at bay. If kids can learn to label which fears are which, they can begin to accept and nourish the fears that keep them safe and tackle the fears that hold them back.

MODEL

Children are notorious for picking up on the mannerisms of others or mirroring behavior they see around them. Oftentimes, this makes adults keenly aware of our bad habits because we begin to see our kids pick up on them. However, if we choose to intentionally model behaviors such as bravery, curiosity, and vulnerability, our children can begin to normalize what it looks like to live in this way. Seeing us choose the unpopular over the obvious, the vulnerable over the comfortable, or the right over the easy sets the stage for our kids to do the same, even when it's scary.

MESSAGE

When referencing messaging in this way, we refer to our ability to cultivate the values our kids are absorbing through many different sources, specifically media like TV, the internet, books, and even the clothes they wear. It's not enough to show kids via the actions of adults; we must also ensure the messaging they're receiving aligns with the strong values and behavior you wish to encourage.

MOTIVATE

Asking kids to adopt new behaviors and stick with novel processes can be difficult. Most likely, if you've interacted with young people at any age, you understand the importance of motivation when it comes to making changes, creating habits, or trying new or scary things. Identifying what motivates your child and how you can use it to support behavioral change will be imperative to utilizing the Four M's. The key, like with many things, is ensuring the motivation is age-appropriate.

For many families, choosing to implement a practice like the Four M's can be a daunting and novel experience. Remembering some important factors will make the process a bit easier:

- Give it time—each step of the practice will happen at its own pace and have its own challenges.

- When you feel it's time to move on to the next step, encourage your child and those around them to keep in mind the good habits you've all learned in the previous steps. This is a progressive and collective process. The steps are meant to build upon each other, not replace each other.

- The intention is best—you cannot read this and expect your family to simply absorb the practice. Deciding to raise kids in this way takes intention, focus, and purpose. Like anything with kids, expect there to be some milestones and some setbacks.

If you, as the rearer of amazing young people, decide to take on the responsibility of forming brave and vocal kids by employing the Four M's, I'm confident you will see the evolution of a stronger, more self-assured, and confident child, ready to use their voice. To dive deeper into the Four M's, including further explanation and practical examples, log on to kristinraeray.com/EmbodyKind

Kristin Ray considers herself a chronic life multi-tasker. She is a children's author, blogger, and public speaker. Early in her career, Kristin took an interest in helping women give power to their voices. In 2016, she founded the sports industry group, Females in Athletic Business. Through that work, she honed her passion for mentoring young women in male-dominated organizations. After starting a family, she departed the sports industry for a role in health care in 2019. Her first children's book, *FEARLESS,* was Amazon's #1 New Release in Children's Short Stories in April 2021. Her follow-up, *Could Girls,* is due out late in 2022 or early 2023. As a survivor of childhood sexual trauma, Kristin is dedicated to intentionally equipping her daughter and girls around the world with the knowledge and power to move through life with confidence. In the Broken and Brave Blog, Kristin focuses on survivors of trauma and the impact trauma has on their ability to parent. She is a passionate speaker on a multitude of topics, including women's empowerment, resilience, intentional parenting, and trauma survival. Kristin is the proud mother of one amazing daughter and wife to a supremely supportive husband. Kristin is a native of Lansing, Michigan, and a graduate of Michigan State University.

Connect with Kristin:

Website: kristinraeray.com

Facebook: kristinraerayco

Twitter: kristinrp27

Instagram: kristinraeray

LinkedIn: Kristin-ray

Email: info@kristinraeray.com

CHAPTER 8

EMBODYING SENSORY SENSE

DISCOVERING YOUR UNIQUE WAY TO THRIVE

Liz Dobbins, PCC, Professional Certified Coach,
International Coach Federation

Imagine a world where everyone could self-regulate and thrive regardless of their surroundings or environment. How would it feel to be able to adjust at a moment's notice, pivot when necessary, and thrive with agility? Each one of us has the opportunity to self-regulate no matter what the circumstance and tune into our unique sensory fingerprint to be at ease and succeed with grace.

The key is to understand how your sensory preferences impact you so you can stay present as you face challenges and navigate life.

MY STORY

I'd like to invite you to a moment in my adolescence where one event, in particular, made an impact on me. In my junior year of high school, the guidance counselor asked me to come into his office to share disappointing news. In a low tone, he said, "After much consideration, Liz, I believe obtaining a job after high school would be an excellent alternative to continuing on to college. College will be too much of a challenge for you." In shock and disbelief, I limped home, stumbled through the front door, and slumped on the couch crying. I felt like my whole world and future had just been wiped away. Sobbing with the raindrops of reality, I poured my heart out to my mom. She took a sip from her cup of coffee and looked up into my eyes with her strong, compassionate gaze, and gently said, "It's not what happens to you, but how you respond to it. So, knowing what you know now, what is your solution?" At that moment, to open up new creative possibilities for myself, I knew I needed to remove my emotions by going for a walk and connecting to my dreams. It was my dream to attend college and excel in sports. The only thing I knew was that I was bound for college, no matter what anyone else thought.

I used a movement ritual when I felt sad, angry, or needed to solve an issue. I take myself away from the situation and walk outside. During this particular walk, I found my solution. In light of the contrasting opinion of my guidance counselor and myself, I went outside and walked around my block five times. I felt my sadness twist and turn inside me while feelings of sorrow and anger started to move with each slow step. Finally, on the fifth time around the block, I felt my steps grow quicker with more purpose. I shifted from feeling sad, lost, and angry into accepting a challenge. At this moment, I was certain I wouldn't be told I lacked the ability in my sports or my grades. This time, entering the front door, I embodied a sense of determination and confidence in my heart and announced to my mother with my head held high, "I will not allow the counselor to tell me how to live my life. I'm going to college and will be a collegiate athlete!" What an insight for me to move emotions.

On my next day at school, I walked into my counselor's office, looked him in the eye, and firmly announced, "My sports are everything to me, and I have applied to a number of colleges. Nothing will get in my way from attending a university to pursue my education and play sports." Then, I turned and walked out of the guidance counselor's office with determination. I decided at that moment that I'd do whatever I needed to do by treating my grades like I was in training for my sports. From this time on, I was committed to achieving my goal. I like to believe that my high school counselor displayed an *act of kindness* that ignited my spirit. I was determined I'd use my love of sports to get into a university where I could excel at both academics and sports together.

This technique of responding rather than reacting continues in my role as an educator, coach, and consultant. I attribute my success and curiosity to my mother's teachings as her voice still rings in my ears every day, "It's not what happens to you but how you respond to it. So, knowing what you know now, what is your solution?" Who knew that my mother had great insight to reinforce, "It's not what happens to you but how you respond," which taught me to take time out to figure out my response.

Coming from my athletic background, taking time out to move with the intention to shift emotion was an easy addition to my daily toolkit. When faced with a challenge, I now automatically take a break before responding. Physically, I will now move to elevate my emotions, whether it's taking a walk, going for a run, or any kind of exercise first.

Another a-ha moment came during my studies in college. When one of my well-known professors, Dr. Jean Pyfer, was conducting research in the Perceptual Motor Clinic on sensory-based activities, I began to connect the dots between my personal experience of using movement to the science of why it works. It has been my experience that doing sensory-based movement activities effectively influence student behaviors and provides a sense of calm and well-being. Furthermore, I observed that specific sensory activities, such as weighted activities against gravity, had a calming effect.

Today, neuroscience demonstrates that each of us has a unique sensory DNA which we can tap into to determine what sensory tools will support our self-regulation. We are thus brought back to the principle of taking time to move our bodies as a vital component of controlling our emotions.

THE PRACTICE

PRACTICAL

Embodying sensory sense means to exist in your body and is referred to as body awareness.

The founder and director of Psycho-Physical Therapy, Bill Bowen, MFA, LMT, informs us that, "The body and mind are mutually interactive and mutually influential," which means the body continually informs the mind of what's going on in the body. At the same time, the mind receives information about the world through our senses. Our senses then relay information from the environment, and our brain interprets this information and then tells us how to react.

One important step is identifying your sensory challenges and preferences. This will allow you to build your sensory tool kit. It's important to recognize that every individual has a unique sensory fingerprint, and therefore, there is no wrong or right in your preference. One event may be a trigger for one individual and may not be a trigger for another.

IDENTIFYING SENSORY PREFERENCES

The following questions are a sample designed to support you in identifying what thriving feels, looks, and sounds like for you. This will help you find clarity on your sensory preferences. Note how you feel about your immediate choices. For example, as you read through, notice if you feel stress, fear or anxiety, or have a feeling of overwhelmed (flooded). Or if you feel energized, engaged, calm, or neutral. There are no right or wrong answers; rather, this is a tool to uncover your unique sensory fingerprint.

How would you describe the environment that you thrive in?

A. Constant change, bright lights, open windows, music, and interruptions may be welcomed
B. Flexible workspace, organized office, enjoy calming music or audiobooks
C. Quiet, noise-canceling earphones, sensitive to light and scents, neat and tidy

Does a workout in the morning energize you?

A. Often energizes me
B. Sometimes energizes me
C. Rarely energizes me

Do you like socializing in large groups?

A. Love being in large groups
B. Flexible in being in a large group or a small group
C. Prefer small groups

What is your reaction to smell?

   A. Prefer to smell essential oils, cologne/ perfume/ air fresheners
   B. Like a variety of odors
   C. Prefer no odors around at all

In general, if you selected mostly A's, you are a Sensory Seeker—referred to as someone with high energy and who likes an active environment for more stimulus. You may prefer to socialize in large groups and are goal-driven.

If you selected mostly B's, you are Sensory Neutral—referred to as someone who is flexible and can easily shift and cope with stress; in other words, goes with the flow.

If you selected mostly C's, you are a Sensory Avoider—referred to as someone who is cautious, does not like change, prefers a calm environment, socializing in small groups, and likes structure.

Movement is a key component to support self-regulation in moving emotion and creates the results that propel us to positive outcomes. I uncovered movement as a tool during my early experience in high school when I needed to shift from discouraged and angry to empowered and confident. Even now, as I reflect, I can see that taking time to walk or exercise before coming up with a solution supported me emotionally in my decisions. Furthering my education in sensory awareness and how my personal sensory thresholds operate and adapt to the environment is learning based in neuroscience.

I've included a few sensory tools below to support you with self-regulation. You can use these movement tools as a starting point for your own sensory tool kit.

Based on your sensory preferences, as you uncovered above, here are a few tools that will support you to live with ease and well-being while thriving.

Sensory Seeker

- Squeeze a stress ball

- Use a standing desk

- Enjoy a one-minute dance party

- Massage (head, body, hands, back)

- Go for a walking meeting outside

Sensory Neutral

- Practice five minutes of quiet time
- Do something regularly that calms you
- Do something regularly that you enjoy
- When stressed, socialize in smaller groups and when relaxed, socialize in bigger groups

Sensory Avoider

- Organize your home and workspace to promote efficiency and calmness
- Put your cell phone on vibrate with the volume low or off
- Use ringtones with soft, calming, and rhythmic sounds
- Listen to calming music through a set of earphones
- Hold conversations in an isolated place in the room or a separate room when in a large gathering

Being present with your sensory preferences, you're able to see new possibilities for how you can control emotion. By using our body and movement, you can shift the emotions that trigger your sensory system and set yourself up for success.

The benefits of sensory self-regulation are key for the following:

- Enhancing your ability to be present and focus
- Communicating effectively across different backgrounds and in different situations
- Thriving in any environment with tools to manage your sensory thresholds and self-regulate at work, at home, and in relationships
- Learning to trust yourself through your body and how you interact with the world
- Clarity on how movement affects your sensory system and every aspect of how you show up in your life.

Are you curious to learn more about exploring your sensory fingerprint and preferences?

Join me to further your sensory awareness, create your sensory tool kit and deepen your experience to live in agility and self-regulate and optimize health, wellness, and productivity.

I'd love to hear from you and explore how I may support you. To inquire about coaching and sensory workshops or to earn ICF CEUs, you can contact me via the following:

Contact

Liz Dobbins, ICF.PCC

Liz@Propeology

Linkedin: https://www.linkedin.com/in/liz-dobbins/

Facebook: https://www.facebook.com/propelogy/

Website: https://propelogy.com

Special Offer: I am offering readers a complimentary laser coaching session. Mention the code EMBODY KINDNESS for your free coaching session with me, Liz Dobbins, ICF Professional Certified Coach. https://calendly.com/propelogy/20min

I am a master of incubating creativity and stimulating minds. I move people from burn-out to built-up and from high anxiety to high-performance!

I help professionals perform at peak levels so they can have less anxiety and be more productive. Go from disengaged to engaged and support individuals and teams to implement tools so that you can monitor your own internal engine to perform at your high-performance lifestyle.

The majority of my experience has been as an educator, high-performance coach, and consultant in K-12 and higher education sectors. Within the journey of teaching, I completed research in the health and wellness department at the University of Kansas and presented at the state and national levels.

As a published author, I promote the importance of human body intelligence. My coaching credentials are held by (ICF) International Coaching Federation and in the sport of triathlon. I served as the president of KCLUB at the University of Kansas Athletic Department and as the chair of the Women's and Age Group Commission of USAT (United Triathlon Association).

As Propelogy, Inc.'s founder and CEO, I serve the industry as a high-performance coach, and educational consultant, in the corporate arena and in the coaching field. Through this work, I empower peak performance through the understanding of how the mind and body interact.

"Movement bridges life moments and human body intelligence."

CHAPTER 9

WALKING THE LABYRINTH

HEALING OURSELVES AND OUR WORLD

Marijo Grogan, LMSW

MY STORY

On our trip north along the Lake Michigan coastline, I wondered if this year's pilgrimage walking the labyrinth might turn out to miraculously alter my life. Like pilgrims across the centuries, my friend Rosemary and I were looking for a way to integrate the painful experiences life had thrown our way in the past few months. We were looking to push the reset button on our lives.

Rosemary, who is a naturally kind person and always there to help anyone in need, had recently lost two friends. Sadness peeked out underneath the broad smile she showed the world. As usual, I was seeking clarity and insight. The mood of the country had shifted. Most everyone admitted to feeling angry, and I was no exception. My skin prickled when I passed yard signs that flew in the face of my own beliefs. Fear showed up as well. I could hardly breathe at the thought of a confrontation with a neighbor or an irate person at the grocery store. I dreaded the day when push came to shove as I competed with another shopper for the last package of chocolate mints.

I knew people had walked labyrinths since ancient times in hopes of finding inner peace and transformation. *Could some of my anger and fear be transformed?* I was willing to give this a try. Passing miles of cherry orchards, we finally reached our destination. By mid-morning, a large group of people had found their way to this site—a half-spiritual, half-tourist destination.

The labyrinth consisted of lavender plants spread out over a good acre forming the traditional eleven circuits geometric design. Rosemary smiled, ready to dive into our pilgrimage journey to inner peace. Yet I held back, consumed by my own frustration. It was easy for me to judge the people invading this place. While mothers shouted and men laughed, I was nearly knocked off my feet as a group of boys raced by, tossing a beach ball between them. I watched as teenagers emerged from the gift shop licking ice cream cones or balancing cherry turnovers and bottles of soda in their arms. They didn't understand the significance of this beautiful experience. I couldn't help feeling angry. It was easy to judge them.

I withdrew from those around me, finding refuge in the shade of an old oak tree. The scent of the earth, the moss, and wild clover began to calm me. I caught my breath and exhaled sharply. It was time for me to let go. *What were those instructions for beginners' breath that the yoga teacher hoped to imprint on our memory?* Breathe in through the nose and out through the mouth to invite relaxation. I took those deeper breaths and felt my body begin to soften. Finally, I was ready to make the journey into the labyrinth winding my way along its circuitous route. First, however, I needed to set an intention.

Help me to know how to meet those who feel like the other.

Help me to know how to act with kindness and compassion.

Unlike a maze, I knew there was no chance of losing my way inside the labyrinth. Instead, I looked forward to finding my way. Stepping out into the warm afternoon sun, I was ready. Inside I joined others spread out along the path. The enticing aroma of lavender drew me forward. Bees danced between the flowers soaking up warm nectar. The low hum of their flight sounded like background music soothing my soul. Content to focus on my breath, I momentarily closed my eyes and moved forward, sensing the next bend in the path. After some minutes, I began to notice those around me, my fellow pilgrims: teens dressed in black, a young mother pushing a baby carriage, an older couple holding on to each other's arms.

Remembering my intention a strong desire arose to release the anger and frustration that absorbed my attention. *Yes, let it happen. I want to let go of this tight chest, these obsessive judgments about myself and others*—repeating this affirmation, my limbs relaxed, and my breathing slowed to a steady pace. The scent of lavender and suntan lotion blended with the moist sweet smells of a nearby hayfield.

It seemed as if the walk would never end. The sun reached its zenith as I wiped the perspiration from my forehead. Then much to my surprise, after turning a bend in the path, I found myself at the center. It was time to rest in the quiet. Others seemed to have the same idea. I closed my eyes and took another deep breath. After a while, like an invitation, a question began to take shape. *What is my heart telling me?* I took some time to savor this question without forcing any immediate answers.

After a while, I was ready to begin the return journey with this question in mind. Winding in and out along the path, I began to sense new energy. It was a relief to recognize my former irritability dissolving. In its wake, I felt gratitude for the day, the sun, the breeze, the children, and my friend Rosemary. I did not experience any earth-shattering revelations emerging from the labyrinth. The clouds did not part, and the angels did not sing. But in the place of my earlier agitation, I felt calm and connected to the life around me, the natural beauty, and even the people.

That evening Rosemary and I found a B&B not far from the lake. My spirits were restored as we flirted with a charming waiter and shared Tiramisu for dessert. The next morning, awake early, I decided to walk into town. On a Sunday morning, the streets were deserted. At the downtown park framed by large maple trees and some flowering shrubs, I came across a slight man with a short blonde beard and a biker scarf tied around his head. He was bent over the frame of his bicycle. All the accouterments of his journey lay spread neatly on the grass: a large water bottle, sleeping bag, halogen light, knapsack, and a few apples. I stopped momentarily to acknowledge his presence. He looked up and smiled.

"I'm getting ready for the next leg of my trip," he announced.

"Oh, where have you come from?"

"Have been traveling cross-country starting from home in Bend, Oregon." "Wow, what an itinerary," I exclaimed with a laugh. "That is amazing."

"Yeah, in this recession, I lost my job as a carpenter. Decided at that moment, it was time to get out of town."

I saw Rosemary coming up the sidewalk and introduced her to the man I now knew as Dan. Together we shot more questions in his direction.

"I've heard Bend is a great place," taking my cue from the music festival that greeted Cheryl Strayed after her 1,000-mile trek along the Pacific Crest Trail. I enjoyed her book *Wild* and saw Dan as a laid-back sort of guy who might be a member of my tribe.

Having made this assumption, I was shocked at what followed. My comment irritated Dan. He let loose with a plethora of insults hurled at people who don't work and are lazy. This included all the migrants who had invaded his town, many of whom were homeless. "They are just sucking the life out of America," he declared.

Immediately I recognized this moment as the one I'd been dreading since the country shifted toward culture wars. I wanted to turn and run. Rosemary stood next to me, a silent yet supportive sentinel. We were both uncomfortable, yet I was determined to reach into my bag of conflict resolution skills and give them a try. *What were those skills exactly?* I recalled that listening, asking questions, and sharing personal stories might help. *Don't we all wish to show up as a real person rather than a poster child for an ideology?*

I practiced listening and sharing a personal story, but Dan wasn't buying any of it. After about ten minutes, I knew it was time to exit but wasn't sure how to put a graceful spin on our departure. I didn't want to run away from Dan. I was beginning to like him. I wanted to show some kindness to this broken man whose hands shook as he spoke. I wondered what trauma he might have faced back home. I wanted him to know that I admired his determination and courage.

"Rosemary and I need to be back on the road ourselves," I shared. Dan stood with his head tilted toward the grass below his feet. "Before we go, however, I just want to say how much I admire you. Not many people could bike across the country." I took another deep breath. Dan was watching me this time. "You remind me of the men that rode the rails during the Depression when there were no jobs." He was listening. "They were courageous. They looked out for each other." I had his full attention now. *How would I bring this to an end?* "They were able to return home after FDR signed legislation that created jobs for everyone." I paused one more time. "I hope this happens for you, too."

As Rosemary and I walked toward the car, Dan hollered after us. He wanted to share something. We turned as he rushed forward, holding out a piece of paper with some writing on it. "Will you follow me on Facebook?" he asked, smiling this time.

"Sure," I replied. I didn't want to admit how poor I was at keeping up with social media. "I'll try my best." In my heart, I felt as if the intention I set at the labyrinth the day before was fulfilled. I felt empowered and alive. Rosemary expressed her admiration, and we sang old Beatles songs on the way home.

The labyrinth was forgotten when the pandemic arrived, which demanded all my attention. Other news followed sparking increased anxiety. Black Lives Matter and then the climate crisis took center stage as fires, floods and hurricanes ravaged the land. I felt myself falling into despair. Then one day, quite unexpectedly, the labyrinth reappeared in my life. I decided to walk in a new neighborhood. As I passed St. Barnabas Episcopal church, a sign out front read "Labyrinth this way." Tucked into a small wooded area among wildflowers and the community garden, I came upon it.

Although I don't recall setting an intention that day, I did feel peaceful as I completed my walk. Somewhere an ancient memory came back to me. I saw my ancestors making a pilgrimage, walking a similar path, not knowing the future but trusting in the process. I felt connected to them. Then I found myself moving forward in time, imagining the day when friends might join me. I envisioned us holding each other's intentions in our hearts. We would each set off with the usual questions on this journey that felt more like a mystery than a destination. By the end, I saw our circle expanding to include even those we thought of as strangers. Together we were moving toward healing both ourselves and our world. I knew the children of the future were counting on us.

THE PRACTICE

WALKING THE LABYRINTH

While it's sometimes difficult for me to maintain a daily sitting meditation practice, I'm relieved to discover the hand labyrinth, a meditation tool I can use any time, anywhere. Consider this practice when you seek clarity about a question or state of being—feeling anxious or fearful? Try tracing the hand labyrinth while breathing deeply. Watch as you reach a deeper state of relaxation or meditation.

Dr. Lauren Artress of the Grace Cathedral in San Francisco (veriditas. org) was among the first people to introduce the ancient labyrinth walk to a contemporary audience. In 1998 Lauren began taking groups on pilgrimage to experience the labyrinth in the French cathedral at Chartres. They were invited to move into the labyrinth with a focus on releasing, resting, and finally inviting and receiving new energy.

Through Veriditas, I was delighted to discover an opportunity to meet with others in a meditation circle based on tracing hand labyrinths. Usually made of wood or ceramic, these can fit easily in one's hand or can be set on a table. The day I joined the circle, a musician played soft Celtic music while we spent about 15 minutes in silence tracing our own labyrinths. I downloaded a photocopy of the 11 circuit labyrinth and traced its path with my finger during the meditation. This turned out to be a wonderful way to expand my loving-kindness practice. You may also wish to play background music with a simple or repetitious melody to relax into the rhythm of the practice.

First, however, find a quiet space and make yourself comfortable. It helps to sit with a straight back, your feet grounded on the floor or in your imagination on the earth. Begin to notice energy flowing through your body and into the earth, where it feels as if your feet are growing roots. You may wish to breathe in through your nose, pause, and then breathe out through your mouth. Follow this pattern for six to eight breaths.

Take time to set an intention. Remember to be kind to yourself. The anger you feel might merely be a sign of your deep commitment to justice. Grief often indicates the presence of a deeply loving heart. You may be called to hold opposite energetic poles until a healing resolution appears.

Ask for what it is you might need at this time. What message is your heart wishing you to reveal to you?

After setting an intention, take a moment to trace the outer edge of your labyrinth in a counter-clockwise followed by a clockwise direction. When you return to the opening in the labyrinth, you are ready to begin your journey. Take your finger and slowly trace the outline of your labyrinth. Continue noticing your breath pattern and matching this to the slow rhythm of your outline tracing.

When you reach the center, take a few minutes to rest in this place. This is your heart space, sometimes called the place of the womb since new energy and wisdom may be birthed here. Notice if there has been any shift in your initial feelings. Allow yourself time to breathe.

As you move back into the labyrinth, feelings of gratitude or love might arise. Try not to judge your experience at this point. You have planted the seed of an intention and watered it with the open-hearted practice of moving through the twists and turns of this inner journey. Allow the fruit of your experience to ripen in its own time.

I often find it helpful to repeat the following Loving-Kindness mantra before and after my labyrinth walk. This was taken from a talk by Joan Borysenko.

> *May I be at peace. May my heart be open.*
> *May I know the beauty of my own true nature.*
> *May I be healed, and may I be a source of*
> *healing for others.*

With the second repetition, I substitute "You" in the place of "I." "May *you* be at peace," continuing the rest of the mantra. Finally, "May *all* beings be at peace, May *their* hearts be open. . ."

The Buddhist monk, *Thich Nhat Hahn*, coined the word "Inter-being" to describe our total inter-dependence on one another. All beings include other species: insects, fungi, plants, and animals. As we face the threat of climate change, we might wish to invite Gaia's consciousness and wisdom into our meditation. Today, scientists tell us that evolution was achieved through cooperation rather than competition. Somewhere along the line, I realize that practicing kindness might be the most powerful tool we have for dealing with the multiple crises facing our world today.

Marijo Grogan is a psychotherapist with a private practice in Ann Arbor, MI. She designs healing, embodied modalities that encompass a communal as well as personal experience. Employing the arts: drama, painting, music, and storytelling, she has created developmental rites of passage models for youth, partnered with the Mexican-American community to create a Day of the Dead Celebration, and promoted the Global Art Project. Marijo has written extensively on the connection between spirituality, psychology, and healing. An editorial of hers was featured on National Public Radio. She is excited to be part of the Pachamama Alliance—Game Changer Initiative, where a group of creatives explores storytelling through the arts as a means of promoting values that are spiritually fulfilling, socially just, and environmentally sustainable. If you're interested in learning more, feel free to contact her. Blessings on your labyrinth journey!

Connect with Marijo Grogan at: marijogro@gmail.com

CHAPTER 10

REALITY RESET

USING SELF-HYPNOSIS TO HEAL AND MAKE POSITIVE LIFESTYLE CHANGES

Jane Ann Trosin, C.Ht.

MY STORY

"What's wrong with you!"

Shrinking, I want to fade into the grey rock next to me.

"What's wrong with you?"

Shrinking, even more, pretending I am the grey rock, nobody sees me.

"What the hell is wrong with you?"

What is wrong with me?

You've all heard this yelled at one time or another, it doesn't matter who said it, or maybe you were the one delivering the message, unconscious of the effect the words are having and maybe even unconscious of the words we're saying, probably because we hear it over and over until we stop hearing it, and it gets embedded into our brains, subconsciously. That is a form of hypnosis. This is where many of our limiting beliefs come in. These are the beliefs embedded into our minds along our life journey through focus, repetition, trauma, and shock. I use hypnosis, and we will utilize self-hypnosis to work through, dissolve and eradicate those self-limiting beliefs.

It's mid-April after a long Michigan winter. It's been sleeting here for three days, and the sun finally peeked out this afternoon. I, like many of the neighbors, took a break to grab some sunshine. The air feels heavy, and I'm enjoying the fresh scent of earth that permeates the air after rain as I get ready to jog up the Hill of Horror (aptly named by our children.) I look up and see a torpedo coming at me. A young boy on his scooter, going over the safe speed limit, is headed my way. *It's too late.* I jump out of the way as I see him losing control, and I think, *o-oh,* and I hold my breath. His scooter stopped as he hit the dirt, but he didn't. He went head over heels into the mud. As I run to help, I'm thinking, *Oh no, is he okay?* And, *how is his mother ever going to get that mud out?* Just as his dad, who is on his phone, yells, "What the hell is wrong with you?" I will take that as my sign that I'm on track with this message, and I tell you, there is nothing wrong with you. There is nothing wrong with anyone, and no one is a mistake.

We can go years believing there is something wrong with us, and in fact, most of us do. After all, no one is perfect, *right?*

Let's start asking:

"What's right with you?" *My body gets bigger, and my breathing deeper as I puff up my chest.*

"Jane, what's right with you?" *Me standing on the grey rock with my superwoman cape on in my superwoman pose.*

"What the hell is right with you?" *Me, on my neon rock, with my big girl pants on, bravely and fearlessly overcoming any challenge and conquering the world.*

Through the practice of hearing something repeatedly, we may, in the back of our mind (our subconscious), start believing it, affecting our health and well-being by internalizing those thoughts, feelings, emotions, and sensations. The more you focus on a particular idea, the more that idea gets written down in your brain, and the more it becomes your reality.

When we align with our true, authentic selves, it raises our energy and vibration, allowing us to be tuned in and tapped into the universe and more apt to recognize the signs and synchronicities directing our path. By addressing our self-limiting beliefs and negative habits and using self-hypnosis, we get out of that unconscious alignment to people, places, and things that are not right for us. They still show up, but now we are able to recognize what is right or wrong for us by using our intuition. When you can change your mind, you'll be able to change your life as well because both have an impact on each other. When we change on the inside, everything on the outside changes, filling our lives with peace, love, and happiness. When we feel good, we do good and are more apt to embody kindness that spills into our home, work, and school lives.

Our beliefs center around ourselves and shape our perception and perspective, ultimately creating our reality. If your reality does not look like you want and desire, you have the ability to reset it and get it.

People come to work with me because they feel stuck and want to change their lives. I asked one of my clients, "Greg, what do you want your life to look like?" He said, "I don't know. I've always pretty much just lived day-to-day. My dad was a pharmacist, so I became a pharmacist. I just went along with my parents and then my wife. Now they are all gone, and I don't have a clue, but my buddy said you helped him, so here I am, hoping you can help me figure this out."

I asked Greg, "What are your interests; what makes you happy? What do you do that causes you to lose track of time? If you had no limitations, what would you do?" We identified an intention with clear benefits, and we began a daily practice of self-hypnosis.

Close your eyes and imagine you have the thing you want. What do you have to give up to get it? Now open your eyes and ask yourself if it is worth it. If it's a "yes," then it's worth going after. If it's a "no," then your "why" isn't going to get you through the doubts and limiting beliefs. You need to work on your "why" or dream bigger. We get accustomed to and accept our limitations, believing we have no control or that they've gotten too far out of control until we stop dreaming of going after our dreams.

We can take steps to heal and correct our self-limiting beliefs by acknowledging them, setting the intention to change, and taking action. These are the limiting beliefs embedded into our minds along our journey through life subconsciously, through focus, repetition, trauma, and shock. I use hypnosis and self-hypnosis to work through, dissolve and eradicate those self-limiting beliefs.

I felt six feet under when someone repeatedly kept yelling my name and shaking me. I thought, *Leave me alone, stop it.* Then another panicky thought: *Something must have happened to one of the children.* The next thing I know, we are in the car headed to the hospital, and I hear my name over and over, and my seat belt is choking me as I try to dig myself out of a heap of chaos, clutter, and confusion. My body feels like someone used it as a punching bag. Then I hear sternly, "Jane, it's you. You are having seizures."

After a long bleak week in the hospital with no answers as to why I had grand mal seizures, I was sent home with enough meds for a horse. I took the meds for a little over six months. When on the meds, I always felt uneasy, on edge, not to mention depressed. I had an itch so deep I couldn't get to it, and in the process of trying, I scratched my skin until I bled. That's when I had enough and weaned myself off, which felt liberating, lighter and brighter. I felt like exercising again, cooking, and art, which helped life get somewhat back to normal. I wrote that one and only seizure off as a fluke; after all, no one in our family had epilepsy. I believed it to be marital stress—fast forward two and a half years when my nightmare returned. I woke up on the cold floor in a cloud of confusion, knowing something was wrong. I thought, *Oh shit, not again, dear God, not again.* We've all woken up having that "not knowing where you are" feeling, and it's frightening. I didn't know where I was nor who I was. I couldn't remember the last several months. Again, I was under extreme stress, which does strange things to the body.

There are times in life when we get to choose to change our lives, and there are times in life when change suddenly happens to us, out of the blue, turning our world upside down, just like the young boy on the scooter.

Before each seizure, I had an ominous dream that someone was in a hospital bed with their head all wrapped up. The second time I had the dream, it stood out, and I again thought it was about someone else. *Always hopeful.* I have realized that when I dream of someone, that someone is usually me. There is a part in each of us that knows everything. I call it my knower or my intuition. Intuition is a link between our human self and a divine source. It's an unbounded awareness within that we can connect with by quieting our minds. I've found that intuition always leads to peace, love, and joy because it comes from the Source, just as we all do. Like most things, the more you trust your intuition, the louder it becomes, and the more you use it, the stronger it becomes.

I do believe everything happens for a reason. We may not know—or maybe we aren't supposed to know—what the meaning is at the moment, but it's there to trip a feeling, jog our memory, and bring us closer to our intuition, our knower, which is always pointing us home. Home is where the heart is, and the heart is at home when you, as an individual, realize your true potential and align with your true authentic self. When we feel good, we do good, and we embody kindness.

This leads me to tell you why doing the practice I included in this chapter is so grounding and helps the awakening process. It clears a space in our minds, a landing strip, to allow the awareness of the signs and symbols, showing us how and when the universe is speaking to us, guiding, directing, and informing, so we can make the necessary adjustments, change, and heal.

Do you want to live a more fulfilling, vibrant, and exciting life filled with confidence and purpose? I have the perfect practice to set your life on a new trajectory. A reality reset for total body, mind, and soul life satisfaction. The intention is your key to focusing mentally upon some action or result with images, feelings, thoughts, and sensations—it's believing in ourselves, with our whole being, all of our senses. I realized I needed the intention to get well, but I also needed to rely on my intuition to guide me, as some things seemed foreign, absent, and just bizarre. Intuition is a key healing ingredient that is deeper, and it requires us to slow down, quiet the mind, and allow our higher selves to come through. It's a short, usually quite clear, and concise message we get in many different ways. Some hear, some sense, some see. Then there are those who just know, and that is our intuition.

My ultimate self-hypnosis practice is a personal transformation tool you can fully immerse yourself into for a total mind upgrade. By learning and doing this practice, we're able to heal and transform our lives by setting and embedding our intentions for getting what we want and desire. Healing and change happen when we feel safe and nurtured. Who else do you feel safer and nurtured with than yourself? After all, there is only one you, and you are the most important person you will ever have a relationship with.

When we begin to think kind and loving thoughts to ourselves, it has a huge impact on the way we feel and behave. Whether you want to kick a habit, elevate your self-esteem and confidence, or get into the best shape of your life, self-hypnosis is a safe technique and a beautiful way to be kind and loving to yourself and brings fast results in just a few minutes a day. The possibilities are endless to reset your reality. It's that powerful. The more you train your mind to focus on the present and the positive, the happier and more peaceful you will be. Self-hypnosis is like recharging your batteries. If your batteries are running low and your reality does not look like you desire, you have the ability to change it with this simple practice that will help you recharge and reset it. If you're new to hypnosis and doing all four of the steps seems a bit much, then choose one and work on that. Then add another step the next day, and so on. Make it yours, and adapt it to you.

THE PRACTICE

What you need:

- Belief (because, believe me, you're going to love this practice.)
- A few minutes, preferably in the morning, is a great way to start your day.
- A quiet place where you won't be disturbed, and you feel safe and comfortable to rest for a few minutes with your hands and feet uncrossed.
- Comfortable clothes and whatever makes you comfortable.
- Music, scents, temperature, incense, essential oils, candle, pillow, blanket, etc.

1. Set an intention:

- For example, "I deserve to be healed, body, mind, and soul in all ways." Or simply, "I deserve to be healed." Even simpler: "I am healed." I like to use the words "I deserve _____", or "I am _____". (fill in the blank)
- Then see, sense, and feel as though the desire is fulfilled.

- Put yourself in the scene of you being your ideal self.
- Set it and get it.
- See yourself from a new point of you.

2. Take three nice, deep, "letting go" breaths.

On the third breath, as you inhale, look up as though you're looking through the back of your eyebrows, then close the eyes down with the exhale, relaxing the eyes. Then just breathe a little deeper and a little slower. Use your powerful imagination to go within. Follow your breath with your attention and allow the energy in your body to settle. It's not about emptying the mind, it's allowing the mind to empty itself. You may think that you're wasting your time or that it won't work, just let them go. You will probably have to make this decision over and over. But, as time goes on, those thoughts will grow stiller until they are finally silent. This is why it's called a practice.

3. Pull healing light into the body.

Think of your favorite color and pull it in through the top of your head with a big ball of sunny, warm, healing light, and allow it to fill your whole body—radiating to every place and space, each muscle, nerve, tissue, and cell. Feel it, sense it and see it covering, healing, and warming the body up to change. You can even push this healing light outside the body to surround and protect it.

4. Anchor your intention.

Install an anchor into the body, mind, and spirit by physically touching two fingers together or a thumb and a finger as you repeat your intention three times in your head. Activate this anchor anytime you need calming. Let me guide you through this reality reset practice with my youtube link.

https://Youtu.be/9dJ93Nespz0

What's important about this practice is the breath. Breathing is what keeps our blood pumping. Blood is what keeps the body alive. Both are essential to keep the heart functioning. The heart is the first organ that develops, and I find it interesting that each one of us is born with a certain number of breaths, so when we slow down our breathing, we're slowing down the aging process. We have control over our breath which will slow down or speed up the heart rate. Breath is life.

> *Breathing is reciting the name of God. The name of God recorded in the original Hebrew Bible is YH WH. Over time the vowels were added. Rabbis noted that the letters YH WH represent breathing sounds when pronounced without intervening vowels. YH (inhale), WH (exhale.) That the very sound we make when we breathe speaks the name of God. When we come into this world, our first word is God, and when we leave this world, our last word is God.*
>
> ~ Rob Bell

To embody kindness toward ourselves, we need to slow down, focus our attention and intention on the breath, and just breathe and believe.

The benefits of self-hypnosis are innumerable. You, too, can harness the power of your mind to reach impossible goals, kick bad habits, and upgrade your mind using my simple, fast working, self-hypnosis practice. How you decide to use this exciting practice to enhance your life satisfaction will cause your friends and family to wonder how you've gained an almost superhuman ability to go after what you want in life and make it happen. The possibilities are endless, and if you want to know more about how hypnosis can revolutionize your body, mind, and soul, please feel free to contact me.

Jane Ann Trosin, C.Ht., is a certified hypnotherapist at Alive2Thrive Hypnosis, a dietitian, personal trainer, class instructor, Reiki Master, and, her greatest accomplishment, mother of three beautiful children.

She is a certified clinical hypnotherapist with extensive training and experience, specializing in self-hypnosis, anxiety control, weight management, and helping people find their purpose. She is a graduate of the Clinical Hypnosis Institute of Michigan and is a member of the Clinical Hypnosis Professional Group and the Michigan Hypnosis Guild. She received her Dietetics degree from the University of Wisconsin Stevens Point. She maintains personal training and class instruction certifications and regularly attends hypnosis continuing education classes to increase the scope of her hypnotherapy practice.

Jane has always been interested in body, mind, soul, and health and works as a clinical hypnotherapist at Alive2ThriveHypnosis. Previously she worked as a clinical dietitian, was a manager of employee wellness programs, and managed fitness centers. She is a great motivator and an expert hypnotist specializing in healing and making positive, productive lifestyle changes. Hypnosis is her passion, and helping clients align their intentions and actions is her mission.

Hypnosis is an amazing tool to help improve your life by eliminating limiting beliefs and negative habits and establishing positive, productive solutions that help to align the body, mind, and soul. Jane combines intuitive healing with hypnosis while working with clients to get to the heart of the issue, quickly finding solutions. Hypnosis works when nothing else does.

Change your mind, change your life! Empower yourself and reach your goals! Reset your reality because your success is her mission!

Contact Jane at:

Website: Alive2ThriveHypnosis.com

Facebook: Alive2Thrive@intuitivejane

Email: Trosin.jane@gmail.com or Janetrosin@gmail.com

YouTube: Alive2Thrive InAbundance

Free: Self-Hypnosis practice link https://youtu.be/9dJ93Nespz0

Instagram: jane_trosin_

TikTok: Alive2Thrive@alive_2_thrive

LinkedIn: https://www.linkedin.com/in/jane-trosin-398496178

CHAPTER 11

UNLOCKING YOUR FULL POWER

HEALING THE INNER CHILD

Jamison Jacobs

MY STORY

EmbodyKind: We live in a world where banter, critique, sarcasm, and put-downs are exalted. We, as a culture, love to pin people against each other and delight at their expense. We look to leaders who are argumentative, negative, and focus on victimhood as a way to unite. To EmbodyKind is to heal, empower, and hold kindness as a choice. Kindness must first begin with yourself, and from there it flows outward.

We are made up of more than each moment that we live, but also the moments we have lived before. Every moment skates on top of our own history of moments, and below are so many interpretations and reactions that while each moment is unique to itself, our experience of reality is built on our history of experiences. While I wish my story was just a story, it's a fundamental story that my identity and life have been built upon. While I wrestled with an experience that shook me to my very core at a very young age, it was the lack of healing that perpetuated and continued to bring the past into the present. If you're looking to free yourself from your past, looking to have your life go differently, or sometimes wonder why you react the way you do, this chapter will assist you in becoming more empowered. If you give it a chance, it will change your life.

THE EVENT

We got inside the small VW bug. My mother cracked the corner window, lit a cigarette, and put on some music. I sat next to her as the lights switched on, penetrating the night. The car lurched forward, the back engine rattling with acceleration, and we pulled out onto the road. It was late; I yawned and settled into the seat. The night air, the music, and the steady vibration of the car all conspired to send me to sleep. After a while, we stopped, and as the car came to a standstill, my eyes opened. "Look, Jamie!" my mom said with enthusiasm as a family of skunks crossed the road before us. "Oh, wow," I responded, my three-year-old finger pointing at them. As we sped forward into the night, my eyes watched the trees pass by my window, a gentle breeze flowed consistently against my face, and with the steady music and vibration, I leaned into my seat, curled up, and fell back asleep.

When I opened my eyes again, I was inside a white room—the walls bare, the floor white, the curtains white. The room was expansive, and I looked at everything through wooden bars. I didn't know where my mom or dad was; the room was empty. After a while, I called out, "Mom? Hello?" I started to panic, and a nurse came in and said, "Oh, you're awake."

The days after seemed like an eternity. The clocks seemed to tick slower, and time felt like it stood still. I didn't see my mom for days, weeks, then months, and the adults conspiring to protect me, shielded me from the fact that my mother may die. Like any good child, I listened in hallways and in the next room, eavesdropping. Some adults spoke, forgetting I was there. It took me years to figure out what actually happened. All I knew was that my father and mother were gone, and I was alone. I felt like a stranger whose life was paused, living with my mother's aunt and her foster children. The days were okay; they kept me from feeling much, but at night my fears surfaced, and I felt so alone. I cried myself to sleep, deeply missing my mom and dad.

A drunk driver had swerved into our lane, and my mother turned the wheel to the right, taking the full impact of the other vehicle. It immediately snapped her leg, crushed the bones in her hand, and glass from the windshield went into her face and neck. It took the jaws of life to free us. Nothing happened to me; my small three-year-old body flew forward, my head hit the dashboard, and I slipped onto the car's floor. I was vaguely aware of sirens and lights and only came to once I was at the hospital. When my mother arrived at the hospital, she told them she had internal bleeding. They didn't believe her, and the next day she slipped into a coma. Unable to handle her injuries, the hospital transported her to another hospital.

Because my parents had recently divorced, my aunt would not let my father take me. I didn't understand this at the time. I just knew that my mom and dad were gone. There was a general concern that my mother wouldn't make it. She weighed less than a hundred pounds and was only five feet tall. After her surgeries, they just weren't sure if she would pull through. While I don't know if anyone told me directly that she would die, I slowly began to believe she had died. After waiting a few months, I finally got to go to the hospital to see her. I didn't know what any of it meant, but when I arrived and saw all these machines around her, I said, "We had so much fun when you were alive." In my three-year-old brain, I had to believe she didn't make it, that she didn't survive. Why else would she not be with me?

Of course, she was alive, and that year I spent Christmas at the hospital. We had a tree in our room, and I slept by my mother's side on Christmas Eve. The journey to healing had only just begun. My mother was wheelchair-bound for a while and had to learn to write and walk again. Glass would occasionally emerge from her neck and face over the years.

There is this phase when growing up, a period of time one believes their parents are superheroes. It's unclear to a child that a parent can't control the world and events. For a time, I was really angry that my mother let that happen to us. I would not let her go to the bathroom by herself. I was so afraid she could disappear in a moment that I clung to her. Of course, I thought she was dead. My mind could not accept that she would choose to abandon me. If my mother was alive, of course, she could stop the accident from happening; she was still a demigod in my world.

The experience shaped my world and relationships to follow. Even as a teenager, if my mom was out late, I'd sit by the window and read the bible.

It was an irrational reaction, but given my past experience, it meant the world was uncertain and that at any moment, people could disappear from my life. I would rather push away closeness or hold it dearly, not having a lot of bandwidth for anything in between.

In my early relationships, I was waiting to be left, looking for what exits to take, all in service of protecting myself. In arguments, that inner child was powerful. He used the intellect and wit of an adult to believe a reaction or fear was justified. I felt myself reacting out of impulse and apologizing later, embarrassed by my own reaction. I had a romantic notion of relationships reinforced by films and books—the idea that there was "a one" that would completely get you, have you, and never leave your side. Looking back, it dovetailed perfectly with that child's view and desire never to be left. Then when things were good, almost something I could rely on, a distance would enter, and the script would be flipped—a combination of neediness and distance all stemming from this one event.

It took me years to realize how much healing that child needed. Given the terrain, my mother needed to focus on her healing, work, and everything to start her life back up, all without the support of a partner, and in the 70s—which was a disempowering time for women.

Our parents are imperfect, they're unable to give us what we need, and that's okay. The problem is when we grow up and expect our partner to heal and raise our inner child. Since our partner has their own experiences layered with their history and past, they are unable to support us in this way. The unhealed inner child lives in a constant state of need, so even appeasing the child doesn't last very long. If you find yourself in behaviors that seem outside your control and notice you communicate out of compulsion, then an unhealed child wound may be running you. Consider that your inner child needs to be healed and gets to be healed.

The child needs love, acceptance, reassurance, and healing. Left unhealed, the child will continue to run the past in the future. Our inner child literally wants others to heal the child, but partners often have no idea of the psychological experiences and are ill-equipped to quell them. Also, the inner child, because the child is unhealed, will continue to be incomplete and will just find something else to focus on, never quelling the grief inside.

You might do everything you can for your partner, indulging the pain from the past, and they still find fault or an area that isn't enough. It's amazing just how many people are walking around living from their unhealed inner child. The only person responsible for healing your inner child is you. Nobody else can heal that part of you. I'm about to give you a key to healing your inner child. It only works if you actually do it, but if you do it, it can dramatically change your life and your relationships. The inner child does not just show up in romantic relationships but rather wherever relationships occur. Sometimes there is more than one inner child of yours that needs to be healed.

Today I'm a coach; I work with executives, leaders, and coaches in training. Coaching is about more than the goals the clients want to generate or the lives they want to live. Often contexts, patterns, limiting beliefs, and past experiences get in the way of a client's results, and we have to coach around what might be in the way. Coaches are not therapists, so we partner with our clients to shift a context, limiting belief, or a past experience. If a client is stuck and has trouble moving forward, we may also recommend therapeutic support.

THE PRACTICE

As a coach, I wondered if this chapter was too therapeutic to include. I have a number of tools I utilize with my clients to have them shift out of their contexts, limiting beliefs, and past experiences to have them powerfully generate new results. While I wouldn't spend a lot of time with a client on the past, I think healing part of yourself helps you be more empowered in the future, and it's often critical to your personal development.

I realize not everyone wants to develop themselves, but the opportunity to shift a part of your life has implications beyond your wildest dreams. As someone who cares deeply about the world, I've always wanted to contribute meaningfully. When I was younger, it was more about taking care of the planet and helping others. Now my belief is that you can't get everyone to agree on much of anything, but when I help shift my client's relationship to themselves, then they care about everything that's meaningful. I have a coach and have generated powerful results in partnership with my coach.

I have developed a meditation that I have used with my clients. I will share conceptually about the meditation here, and at the end of this chapter will be a link for you to listen and go through the meditation yourself. It's a guided meditation, and all you need is a quiet space to listen and begin to heal your inner child. The first thing to be done is to find the right setting. This meditation should not be done in a car or in a place of travel, but rather within your home. Find a place that is sacred to you, like your bedroom. There may be some tears, so make sure you're in a place you feel comfortable crying.

The meditation itself is fairly simple. That said, I used other people's meditations for years, but they just weren't very good. This meditation is designed for you to go find that inner unhealed part of you and come away with he/she healed. I assert that you know everything you need to know. If there are buried memories or pain, you may want to do this exercise with a therapist. The meditation works best if you know or feel you know the inner child that is still mad, sad, or upset. Also, think about how old they are. This is you angry at three, or sad at five, or mad at six. Whatever the age, go find them. My three-year-old me was still sad/upset, and also, my second-grade self was very mad. The two pain points caused me to act out at times beyond how I wanted to show up. Going back and healing those parts of myself was powerful. Once your eyes are closed, and you're in a relaxed state, you'll be guided by some music. There will be some relaxation exercises to get you comfortable and holding an inner space.

You'll then find your inner child, wherever they are in your imagination, wherever they hang out. My three-year-old hung out in a field and loved to play there. Imagine the scene, the day, calling your child over to you. You spend some time in the energy of the smaller you, and at some point, you will sit. You will ask your inner child to sit in your lap, and you'll ask them: "What do you need?" You will let whatever comes up come up. You'll give your inner child exactly what he/she needs by being with them, embracing them, and really "Embodying Kind." Consider that on some level, you have abandoned little you, who needed some things along the way. The inner child will speak to you as a child—their wants, desires, sadness, and confusion. It's an opportunity to be with them and honor their importance in your journey. The meditation goes on, but that's the overview. I often have to listen to a meditation before I will do it, so I wanted to share the overview.

After doing this meditation, I recommend you do some journaling each morning. After a few nights of sleep, the healing will move into your unconscious, and you will find yourself less triggered and with greater facility over yourself. You may still feel an impulse towards an old pattern, but your inner child, having been healed, won't react strongly. Your relationship with yourself will bring a higher state of happiness and comfort. If it's a deep wound, you may have to repeat this every week but give it some time to move into your body and be patient with yourself. You may also notice other unhealed versions of yourself, so go back as needed.

EmbodyKind is an opportunity to share some experiences that shaped my world and how connecting with myself more gently helped me show up more powerfully and connected in the world.

For a copy of the meditation, go to jjacobscoaching.com/meditation

Please feel free to share your experience.

Jamison Jacobs is a Program Coach for Accomplishment Coaching, an ICF accredited year-long coach and leadership training program. He is also the founder of JJacobs Coaching, which works with executives and leadership teams to more effectively lead in their careers and lives. Jamison lives in Boston, Massachusetts, and has three amazing kids, Kennedy, Liberty, and Lincoln. He enjoys writing and making a difference in the world.

Connect with Jamison here:

https://www.linkedin/in/jamisonjacobs/

https://www.jjacobscoaching.com

CHAPTER 12

THE ART OF KIND-ZEN

MAKING KINDNESS OUR DAILY CUSTOM

Ari Weinzweig, Co-Founding Partner,
Zingerman's Community of Businesses

MY STORY

You will likely know the Japanese concept of *kaizen*. It formally means "change for better" and is used around the world, and here at Zingerman's, as well as part of the very effective approach to continuous improvement that's justifiably gained fame through *The Toyota Way* (thank you, Dr. Liker) and LEAN management. I'd like to build on that innovative work and propose that we capitalize on the concept of kaizen by creating a constructive cultural corollary that I've imagined we might call "kind-zen." In the same way that kaizen practices can help elevate the quality of our work, alter our approach to life, and enhance the quality of all we do, I've come to believe that kind-zen could help take our organizational culture and communities towards a better, more inclusive, respectful, gentler, positive place.

For the last four or five weeks, we've had an old cream-colored school bus parked on the south side of the Roadhouse. Her name is Bertha. She was born in the year 2000, and she belongs to Dr. Peter Glatz, his wife Ann, and their terrific little black and white terrier, Toulouse. On each side of

Berthabus, there's a sign that states calmly, "Make America Kind Again." As you'll quickly see if you look up his story online and if you're lucky enough to meet him in person, Peter Glatz's life is very much congruent with the message on his bus. Every interaction I've had with him has exemplified kind-zen.

After their visit with us, Peter, Ann, and Toulouse will head north for a cooking job he had lined up at a very special, summer season-only, small inn in Northern Michigan. I hope they come back to visit again soon. Their kindness, the message on the bus, and their calm, caring energy have all been wonderful blessings to the Roadhouse, the Zingerman's Community of Businesses, and Ann Arbor, Michigan. I have a feeling that if you come to stand in the space where the bus was, you'll feel the kind spirits that have been gathered there over the last few months filling your own soul. In an homage to Bertha, Doc Glatz, Ann, and Toulouse, I started to wonder— *what if we took Bertha's message and did what we've done so many times now over our years here at Zingerman's—begin with a beautiful concept and turn it into a repeatable recipe, and call it "The Way of Kind-Zen?"*

There's been a lot of talk of late about how American society would better shift towards civility. Compared to killing and active hate, civility is a big step up. I agree. But somehow, for me, civility is not enough. Civility seems like a cease-fire. The same goes for politeness. While it's not a bad thing, superficial politeness to paper over anger and hate isn't going to help anything. Kindness, by contrast, is purposeful and proactive. It's not just the absence of criticism. It's about active connection and meaningful caring. My friend, minister, bacon-lover, Canadian, author, and all-around good guy, Darryl Dash, shared this quote with me from Aaron Menikoff's *Character Matters:* "Kindness is the presence of compassion and generosity toward others. The kind person is helpful, useful, and lovingly working for the well-being of others. . .Kindness exists for the benefit of others."

I understand that kindness on its own won't fix the centuries-old systemic issues that underlie so many of our struggles. Racism will still be wrong. Women's pay inequity will still need to be resolved. The hierarchy will still be harmful. Patriarchy will remain a problem. Divisive politics will still be difficult to deal with. And the long-standing systems that support all of these won't have gone away. I'm not suggesting kindness will cure all ills—many people have been victims of direct and indirect violence and need to find ways to be safe and stand up for themselves. But I do believe that, while we're working to make all that better, kindness would be the beginning of a meaningful difference. As Mahatma Gandhi said, "In a gentle way, you can shake the world."

THE PRACTICE

With all this in mind, I came up with six kinds of kindness to pay attention to.

1. Kindness to Those We Love

This seems like an obvious place to begin the practice of kind-zen. And at first thought, it seems like it *should* (there's the clue that it's not) be easy. We often act out our anger and anxiety on those we're the most emotionally attached to. Approaching each new day with our loved ones as if it's our third date in a budding new relationship or the ninth day of a new job seems like positive constructs to use. It keeps us in a place where we're working hard to be positive and prove our worthiness. Taking those we love for granted isn't good. Treating them badly is worse. By contrast, small kindnesses, continued daily for years, both at work and home, for our partners, longtime coworkers, our family, and our good friends, go a long way to helping our colleagues, customers, suppliers, and neighbors feel the love we have but sometimes hide.

2. Kindness to Those We Don't Agree With

To actively work to be kind to those who say things I don't agree with, who behave in ways that don't work well for me, or believe in things I don't believe isn't easy for me. This can be, for example, people whose political sway is different, who eat food I wouldn't eat, or work in ways we don't want to work. It's easy for any of us to bluster or speak angrily secondhand about someone we'll never meet. Paul taught me 40 years ago to try to learn to disagree without being disagreeable. Kindness can make connections and bridge gaps that anger would turn into chasms.

3. Kindness to Those We Know

It's easy to take those we work with every day for granted; to forget to say thanks to our IT departments, the people who process our payroll, and the people who deliver our produce every morning. And yet, I believe active kindness inserted regularly into our equations can only help enhance the richness of our cultural connections. At Zingerman's, this is often our Three Steps of Giving Great Service. Everything from buying the coffee for the friend behind you in line to sending heartfelt thank you notes.

4. Kindness to Those We Don't Know

If we're all—as I believe—living in the same ecosystem, and if every small action impacts the ecosystem in meaningful ways, then I begin to wonder how much good could come if acts of kindness to our fellow community members were to become our norm. "Helping Kids Rise," writing in Medium, says, "One small act of kindness can change the world, and one book can be the spark that ignites that act of kindness." (If you want to read about one really small and wonderful act of kindness that Kim Green at the Roadhouse did for someone she didn't really know, and a dog named Sugar, see page 432 in *Zingerman's Guide to Good Leading, Part 3; A Lapsed Anarchist's Approach to Managing Ourselves*. It won't fit here, but if you want, send me a note at ari@zingermans.com, and I'll email you the story.)

5. Kindness to the World

Someone taught me a long time ago that one could generally judge a person's demeanor by how they treated animals. I realized later that the better saying shouldn't be "Beware of dog"—it's "Beware of people who take their anger and rage out *on* dogs." My friend was right. The way we treat animals seems to almost always be a direct reflection of how we're likely to treat other humans. The same extends to the world as a whole. Sustainable farmers, I realize, treat their plants kindly. Good cooks bring love to the ingredients—they consistently cook with kindness, and you can taste it in the quality of what they cook. Showing kindness to the planet can only help.

6. Kindness to Ourselves

I learned the hard way and then wrote about it in the "Managing Ourselves" essay in *Zingerman's Guide to Good Leading, Part 3; A Lapsed Anarchist's Approach to Managing Ourselves* that how we talk to ourselves is a big deal. If we don't start with kindness to ourselves, we will fail consistently to convey respectful kindness to others. This can be easier said than done. As artist Anne Truitt said, "It takes kindness to forgive oneself for one's life." Ultimately this may be the most difficult of the six to master. We can use rigor and regimen to help. As Julia Cameron suggests, each time you take a conscious breath, take a moment and "Ask yourself how *you* are feeling. Listen to your answer. Respond kindly."

Having laid out this kind-zen construct, I'm going to challenge myself to do each of these daily. And if that turns out to be easy, then I'll double down and do each one twice. And then maybe three times. If we do, we will surely live up to our name as members of human*kind.*

I realized in writing this that kindness doesn't have to be casual—we can construct systems around it too. What if, on the odd hours of each day, we were reached out and did an act of kindness. Every day (depending on when you get up and go to bed), at 7 a.m., 9 a.m., 11 a.m., and 1 p.m., we do an act of kindness. Even if we all only did six a day, and there are 100,000 people living in Ann Arbor, that would be—no joke—over half a million a day! If the whole town could keep it up for the whole year, every day, which honestly doesn't seem that hard, my math says it would get us to 219,000,000 acts of kindness.

To illustrate a bit of this all-in-real-life action, here's a snippet of a sidebar on this subject taken from *Zingerman's Guide to Good Leading, Part 3; A Lapsed Anarchist's Approach to Managing Ourselves:*

Act In Kindness

"Kindness is free. 'That's what I said to a schoolroom full of 1st and 2nd graders a few years ago. It just sort of came out of my mouth. I think I was probably more nervous talking to those 100 or so little kids than I am presenting to five times as many upper-level business executives. I don't have kids myself, and I had a hard time figuring out what a shy CEO was supposed to tell a bunch of six and seven-year-olds. I ended up just sharing my personal story and encouraging them to be themselves, to learn a lot, and work hard at whatever they want to do. I shared my belief that it's totally normal to want to be mad at your sister or your parents or the teacher or some kid on the playground. And then, at the end, I added in what just happened to pop into my head: The best way to make the world a better place is just to be kind to everyone around you—kindness is free.'"

As Lao-Tzu told it, "Kindness in words creates confidence. Kindness in thinking creates profoundness. Kindness in giving creates love." You can put kindness to work anywhere you want: tip big, smile broadly, open doors, let someone get in front of you in line, and stop cutting off every driver who radiates rudeness to show them who's boss. Simply sending a few more thank-you notes, assisting seniors in crossing the street, and helping parents with strollers squeeze through doorways works wonders.

While I was writing the original draft of this essay a few years ago, we sent a scone and a cup of coffee out to a driver waiting by his limo while the VIPs he was transporting were inside the deli ordering sandwiches. I don't share the story because we're so special; only because it's a real-life example of an incredibly easy, inexpensive way to put generosity into action. I mean, why not do something nice for the guy? As you might imagine, he was pretty excited. And so was Elin Walter, who worked at the deli then and brought it out to him. When I mentioned something to Elin about taking the driver something as a gift, she reacted as if it were the most normal thing in the world and got on it immediately. Generosity is well ensconced in our culture.

While all this theory may be inspiring, the important thing is to do it. Kindness is free, and it's actually almost covert—no need to announce a new program or engage anyone else. You could try it right now. Put the book down (you probably need a break anyway) and find someone, in person, online, or on the phone, someone you know or someone you've never met, and do something small but meaningful for them. If you want to do this at an advanced level, find a person with whom you share tension in your relationship (we all have them) and do something nice for them right now. I guarantee that you'll get good results.

I've been using this principle of late when I teach time management. To show how much good can come from a single, often wasted minute, I ask people to take out their phones and text someone they know to thank them. The only guideline is that the thank you has to be sincere. And specific. Within minutes, responses start coming back. There is an occasional "Why are you telling me that? Are you ok?" (Remember—when you pour water onto really dry soil, at first, it just runs right over the top.) But 99 percent of the responses are positive, and some tear-provokingly so. If you want to completely seal the spiritual deal and you're driven by data, Adam Grant's research shows that doing five generous acts one day a week will get you the best emotional energy boost (better than doing one a day). Apparently, this practice builds a reservoir of goodwill and positive energy that stays with us for the rest of the week.

As I was working on this piece, I kept thinking about my friend, the artist Takara Gudell. Sadly, I know her beloved brother, Kevin Eric Bethea, passed away in April 2019. I'm sad and sorry that I never got to meet Kevin. Every time Takara talks about him, she says how kind he was. Here's what she shared:

> "My brother Kevin Beathea. He was so kind and considerate. You would've loved him—music genius, played the trumpet, he and I were lovers of the woodwinds. I always felt safe around him. He was my protector, always far away and still close enough. His kindness started when he was young. Pre-teens grocery shopping for the elderly in our community. His kindness wove the siblings together—always listening and seeing ahead of the curve. His eyes were soft and curious, and his tone stable. At 6'3, while he may appear as a threat to some, others sighed and quietly smiled when he walked into a room. Peace entered. He was a gentleboy that became a gentleman. Kindness is subtle. Kindness is quiet. There are days I just sit in his kindness and smile."

If we practice kind-zen regularly, make it a way of life and a way of working, our worlds can only get better. If we follow Takara's lead, built on Kevin's life, what if we could sit daily, in each other's kindness, and smile?

Kahlil Gibran famously said, "Work is love made visible." The phrase "Practice random kindness and senseless acts of beauty" was coined by

Anne Herbert, who wrote it on a restaurant placemat in 1982, the very same year we opened the deli. When I put all that together in my head, I started wondering if maybe we at Zingerman's could aspire to be "kindness made tangible"... to take our already kind organizational culture and make it even kinder. Since, as Peter Block says, "You only teach what you need to learn," I wrote this piece, I know, as much for my own learning, self-improvement, and guidance as anything else. It has already helped to make kind-zen a part of my daily practice. I hope it will be of help to you as well.

Ari Weinzweig is CEO and co-founding partner of Zingerman's Community of Businesses, which includes Zingerman's Delicatessen, Bakehouse, Creamery, Catering, Mail Order, ZingTrain, Coffee Company, Roadhouse, Candy Manufactory, Events at Cornman Farms, Miss Kim and Zingerman's Food Tours. Zingerman's produces, sells, and serves all sorts of full-flavored, traditional foods in its home of Ann Arbor, Michigan, to the tune of $68,000,000 a year in annual sales.

Ari was recognized as one of the "Who's Who of Food & Beverage in America" by the 2006 James Beard Foundation and has been awarded a Bon Appetit Lifetime Achievement Award, among many recognitions. Ari is the author of a number of articles and books, including *Zingerman's Guide to Good Eating, Zingerman's Guide to Better Bacon (Zingerman's Press), Zingerman's Guide to Giving Great Service, Zingerman's Guide to Good Eating (Houghton Mifflin), Zingerman's Guide to Good Leading, Part 1: A Lapsed Anarchist's Approach to Building a Great Business, and Zingerman's Guide to Good Leading, Part 2: A Lapsed Anarchist's Approach to Being a Better Leader. Zingerman's Guide to Good Leading, Part 3; A Lapsed Anarchist's Approach to Managing Ourselves. Zingerman's Guide to Good Leading, Part 4; A Lapsed Anarchist's Approach to the Power of Beliefs in Business* was released in the summer of 2016. In 2017 Ari was named one of "The World's 10 Top CEOs (They Lead in a Totally Unique Way)" by Inc. Magazine. In 2018 he released the pamphlet, "The Art of Business; Why I Want to be an Artist." Another pamphlet, "Going into Business with Emma Goldman," came out in June 2019. "Humility; A Humble, Anarchistic Inquiry" came out in October 2020. His most recent pamphlet, "Working Through Hard Times; Life and Leadership Learnings from 2020," was published in the first weeks of 2021.

CHAPTER 13

THE GIFTS IN OUR TRIGGERS

LEARNING YOUR BODY'S SIGNALS FOR HEALING

Krysta L. O'Neill

MY STORY

"Your face changed to complete anger; I ran up the unfinished plywood stairs, followed closely by you. You began to hit and scratch me with everything in you. Despite the look on your face and the anger you projected towards me, I could not help but laugh the entire time."

This was my younger brother's account of a trigger I had when I was 13. My life at this point had more childhood trauma than happy family dinners. When my triggers happened in a family dynamic that included four brothers, teasing became the primary family language. I tried to hide them to bypass the teasing, and yet they'd still come.

Is there something wrong with me? Why do I get triggered?

The amount of anger and rage inside me didn't seem normal. I constantly heard things like, "Oh Krysta, she's so sensitive," or "Don't get her mad she will claw your eyes out." My triggers became a joke, and I became the greatest people pleaser and good girl I could be. I tried to shove them down only to find them rear their ugly heads even louder when I was an adult.

My dad was of the belief that women should be seen and not heard, cook dinner, raise the children, and keep the house clean. His first three children were boys, and he had that down pat. He could handle them, and when they got out of line, he took them to the basement and had them pick out a piece of kindling wood for their beating. I once took the fateful walk downstairs; I had received a C on my report card in fourth grade, and it was my first time being told to "Go pick out your stick."

Being the good girl, I did as I was told, went downstairs, and then the trigger and emotion came. I knew my dad would not respond to anger (especially from a woman), and my response was a full-on sob. I cried so hard he sent me back upstairs without a beating. This time the trigger worked to my advantage, and my brothers, although relieved I didn't get a beating, still showed their wrath due to the lack of equality. They knew crying would never work for them.

My mother, at this point in my life, was mostly numb or absent. Her alcoholism took hold of her life, and the beautiful, stay-at-home mother with six children numbed herself to a place where she was unrecognizable. She left for weeks at a time when my dad drove cross country as a Teamster truck driver. My oldest brother and I did our best to keep the household working so my dad would not know she had left. These were the days before GPS and cell phones.

My dad eventually won custody of my siblings and me, and he hired a neighbor's sister to come and live with us and be our live-in housekeeper. That's what we called her. While it was stable and supportive, we were now being raised by someone else with different values and traditions—different everything. And my mom and dad were not easily accessible. We eventually churned through many housekeepers. I don't remember much of that time. I do recall that I ended up in the hospital for seven days with pneumonia. I lost almost 28 pounds and did not complete seventh grade. It was after this, when I was starting to heal, that my family split apart into fractions of who we used to be.

The younger three children, including myself, eventually went to live with my mother and ended up in foster care for periods of time. The older three became emancipated, renting their own house, while some completed high school. For decades, my mother's primary relationship continued to be alcohol. My dad started life over four hours away in northern Maine with a new marriage that produced two daughters.

The toxic stress grew in me; I could not understand the abandonment of my father, but I was taught not to question him. I could not understand why my mother would choose alcohol over her children, time and time again. My mother would get so mad because I did not want to go to Ala-non. She desperately wanted to be understood and yet had no credibility because she was still actively drinking. She would say, "Alcoholism is a family disease. I'm an alcoholic; I have a disease. You wouldn't be this mad at someone with cancer, would you?"

My life was filled with confusion, and the good girl became my identity. The silent rage unconsciously churned in my belly. Living without my siblings was one of the hardest things to handle as a teenager. We lived in neighboring states, and I longed to be back in my childhood home with them. We saw each other as often as we could and missed each other dearly.

As I got older, I felt a lot of shame around my triggers. I felt broken. I did all the therapy and worked to try and uncover where they came from and how to release them productively. Yet still, the triggers came and were met with whatever power I had to resist and control them. Relationships became hard when I could not control the triggers and when it was that time of the month, it would be noticeably worse. I tried vitamins, diets, therapy, religion, spirituality, education—anything to try and fix myself.

As I continued to grow as an adult, I continued my journey of healing my triggers, and life gave me plenty of opportunities to practice. At 29, my life stopped when my first-born son died 36 hours after he was born. It was unknown throughout my entire pregnancy that he had Autosomal Polycystic Kidney Disease. I experienced the death of my very best friend and sister-in-law at 40 years old unexpectedly. I found out I had Endometriosis that caused infertility and subsequent rounds of in-vitro fertilization that did not produce a pregnancy (thankfully, we were blessed with a miracle son who showed up in his very own time). And there was the breakdown of my marriage to the love of my life and current husband that we were thankfully able to repair together.

For every reader that has experienced even one trigger in their life, I'm sharing the tool that has worked to support me in healing. There is tremendous comfort and healing in knowing the signals in our bodies and being able to find the gifts in our triggers.

THE PRACTICE

LEARNING YOUR BODY'S SIGNALS FOR HEALING

First, you must know you are not broken!

The definition of "trigger," as it relates to this tool, is an awakening of a past unhealed inner wound that most likely occurred before the age of 12. This awakening causes your brain to go into a fight, flight, or freeze response. And in my case, add-in, "Fuck you!"

You will need a journal and a pen.

First, know your body:

1. Bring to mind the last time you experienced a trigger. Take note and write down in your journal the answers to these questions:

   What were the physical sensations in your body?

   Where in your body did you feel them?

   What was the temperature in your body? Do you get abnormally cold or flushed and warm?

   What were your thoughts? Was your mind racing, were you focused on one thought over and over, or were you thinking of multiple thoughts, unable to focus?

   Write down all physical sensations, and know these are your body's warning signals that a trigger is coming on.

2. Find your feet, stand confidently, and find yourself on this earth. Where are you? Your body is reacting to fight, flight, or freeze. Fight, flight or freeze is a response to fear. First confirm: Are you in danger? If you're in danger, take the appropriate action for safety. If you're not in danger, take notice of your physical location, your address, or geography at the time. The intention of this is to ground you, and if you can do this barefoot on the earth, even better. This grounding is always available to you.

3. Bring to mind the belief inside of you that was causing the trigger. Not the current situation or what got you upset, but the belief activated in your body's operating system. This can take some time

to navigate through. For example, if your friend is late and you have a history of always waiting for them, and today it's causing a trigger, the belief inside you may be: My time doesn't matter, or, I don't matter. Another example is if your partner is upset with you because you didn't (insert complaint). The belief inside of you may be, I'm not good enough, I am not enough, or even, I'm unlovable.

4. Take the identified belief and think back to when you first experienced that belief (this is most likely before the age of 12, the younger, the better). For example, "When I got a C in English in fourth grade, my dad got so angry, he planned to punish and beat me, and I believed that I was not good enough."

5. Take some time to journal and meditate with your younger self. In my example, it was my fourth-grade self. Close your eyes and see yourself at that age; recall what you looked, smelled and felt like, the time of the year it was, and where you were when this happened. When you have this memory alive, imagine the adult you with your younger self. Share how much you love this part of you, and reassure them that you will always be here for them. Ask them, "How can I support and love you right now?" And in your mind's eye, do just that—care for them as you would today and let that part of you know they matter. When you're complete, let them know when you're triggered in the future, you will come back to them and meet them where they are and reassure them that they're loved. Welcome, that part of you that is now acknowledged and nurtured into your heart. Take three deep breaths and open your eyes.

6. Take out your journal and fill one full page or more with this experience. Answer the following questions: What did you need that you can now give to yourself? What is a new belief you can adopt and operate from when you feel the onset of a trigger? Practice operating from that new belief.

If you'd love more tips on how to find the gifts in your triggers, please head over to https://letterstolegacy.com to learn how to document your legacy, wake up to the gift of who you are, and operate from a creative belief.

Krysta Lee O'Neill is the founder of Letters to Legacy, an organization designed to document our individual legacy and gift. She is an ontological coach focused on generating self-love and generational healing. With a vision to turn her pain into purpose, she believes as one person heals, those around them heal exponentially. She shares her experience of navigating through shame with grit and determination to inspire and empower those around her. She is fierce in her passion for healing and deeply tender in love and empathy with anyone she meets.

She keeps joy alive in her family by visiting their favorite spot in Aruba and treating their family dogs, Norman and Phillip, as humans. In the fall, you'll always find her at a football game cheering on her husband coaching or son playing every weekend. When she takes a pause, she can be found at any random park on a swing letting her hair flow in the wind and reflecting on her journey.

Connect with Krysta:

Website: https://krystaoneill.com/

Organization website: https://letterstolegacy.com/

Facebook: https://www.Facebook.com/krystamurrayoneill/

Twitter: https://www.Twitter.com/krystaoneill/

Instagram: https://www.Instagram.com/krystaoneill13/

LinkedIn: https://www.linkedin.com/in/krystaoneill/

CHAPTER 14

SACRED HOOP HEALING

INVOKING PERSONAL TRANSFORMATION ONE REVOLUTION AT A TIME

Tisha Marina Bernard, MA, Coach/Therapist,
Educator, Ancestral Medicine Practitioner

MY STORY

The sacred hula hoop was brought into my life to teach me many lessons, including not to give up. Over time, it became an essential tool to help me navigate through my depression and anxiety. It also taught me to practice compassion and kindness toward myself. My first epiphany came one night when I realized the formal term for the hoop spinning in a circle was a revolution. What I observed in physical form was also happening within me, my own personal revolution. The hoop was changing the way I saw myself and the way I operated in the world. I came to see that when I shared the sacred hoop with others, a revolution of humanity could take place.

I will never forget the moment my life changed. When I saw them, everything seemed frozen in time. Even though the party was loud, suddenly everything went silent for me. It was as if a spotlight came on and highlighted only two bodies, with all the other people just gone. My body began to fall into a trance. I had never seen anything like this in my entire life. I wasn't exactly sure what was happening, but I knew I was changed forever. There was no turning back. I simply had to do what they were doing. But what *were* they doing? They were dancing, yet they were dancing with a circular object. This circle seemed to move everywhere, from the tops of their heads to their knees, to their feet, to—wait—their head? Again? *How is this even possible?*

I watched, mesmerized, wondering for a moment if maybe they were hypnotizing me. Slowly, I began to hear the music and the chatter of the people. The dancers stopped, and I slowly felt myself come back into my body. I felt as if I was on a mission. I walked directly up to them and asked, "What are you doing?". With huge smiles on their faces, they replied, "We're hoop dancing." They handed me a hula hoop, and I stepped into the circle. That circle felt awkward as it went around my body, and then it fell to the floor. I couldn't imagine how this circle was moving all over the body of these other dancers while mine just fell to the floor. But what I *did* know was that I wanted, no, I *needed* my own hula hoop (which had now become a sacred hoop). I knew once I had one, nothing could stop me from doing all the amazing tricks that these two women had just performed. These hoops looked like no other hoops I had seen before, and I knew I had found something truly special. "How can I get a hula hoop like yours?" I asked. "Give us a call," they told me. I could hardly contain my excitement at the prospect of getting my first hoop.

The next day, I went to the toy store and purchased a plastic hula hoop (not yet aware that these versions were not the same as the one I had just used the night before). I could barely contain my excitement driving home. I ran into my living room and started hooping, but it just kept falling to the ground. It simply would *not stay up*. I was devastated and immediately began to doubt myself. *How were these women doing such graceful tricks with such ease?*

I called them. "Can I buy a hoop?" They invited me over, and I learned that their hoops were handmade from PVC pipe. They were much bigger and heavier than the small plastic hoop I had just purchased from the toy store. I tried out my new hoop, and it went around my waist with ease! This was the magic of having a proper hoop. I thanked them with sheer joy and went back home to play. Little did I know, the life-changing journey this new, sacred hoop was about to take me on.

My friend also bought a hoop, so I went over to her house to play. My friend seemed to master it immediately. Me, not so much. Mine kept falling, making me feel so clumsy. We practiced together every day for weeks. One night, I decided hooping wasn't for me. I was completely ready to give up. That night, with a crushing sorrow in my heart, I picked up the hoop one more time. I decided then and there that if it didn't work *this* night—I was giving up. I felt foolish, and every negative thought I had about myself seemed to creep in every time I picked up that hoop for one more revolution. Then, I decided to put on my Missy Elliot, my favorite hip-hop artist, and just began to dance. Suddenly, it was like someone touched me *and* my hoop together with a magic wand. The hoop suddenly seemed to stay on my waist, not falling to the ground. Together, we danced into the wee hours of the night.

I was hooked.

Immediately, I noticed myself waking up earlier in the morning just so I could hoop. For me, this was huge. I'm not a morning person, and waking up is often the hardest thing to do. I felt my hoop whispering to me, "Come play." I happily obliged. By then, my friend and I were hooping every day, so we decided to take our practice down to Venice Beach, California, and set up on the performer's sidewalk. We set up our stereo, a small bucket for tips, and then we *rocked out.* We quickly gathered attention (and generous tips) and ended up performing for the entire summer. One day, a woman approached. "Can I buy a hoop from you?". I immediately said, "Yes," and we exchanged numbers. Of course, I had never made a hula hoop before, so my next thought was, *I'd better figure out how to make hoops!* It was this practice of saying yes to an opportunity that propelled me to bring the sacred (hula) hoop to others. I reached out to the woman who had originally sold me the hoops I was using and learned how to make hoops from her. Before I knew it, I was selling my hoops and making a nice income on the side.

Then, my chronic depression kicked in. This debilitating depression often stops me from living my life and has been one of my longest and most challenging journeys. Depression challenges my faith with my spirituality, and I feel all alone. Despite these challenges, I still found the energy and strength to hoop. There were times I'd cry the entire time I was hooping, but I kept on going. I began to understand that this was a sacred circle and a tool for healing. The hoop was now my best friend and something I could lean on in dark times. Nothing in my life had ever inspired me in this way, so I decided that I wanted to share this transformative circle with others. I made several hoops and brought them to my after-school program.

At the time, I was the director of a dance program for at-risk youth in the inner city of Los Angeles. I worked with youth who dealt with violence, drugs, and gangs daily. Dancing became the art that brought us all together. I prepared for class by simply laying all the hoops out on the floor, putting the kid's favorite music on, and waiting for them to enter the classroom. I was nervous they would think the hoops were silly and would laugh at me for bringing them. Instead, what I saw happen next was pure magic. The kids ran into the room and started playing with the hoops. Some would loop them around their waist to hoop. Others would roll them around or throw them back and forth to each other, like a ring toss. They came up with ideas I never thought of. I sat back and witnessed young people who often had to behave like adults simply to survive, go back to *just being kids*—as the room filled with laughter, my eyes filled with tears.

Wanting to continue my journey to share the joy of this sacred hoop, I brought some hoops to a Fourth of July party. Once again, I simply laid the hoops out in the backyard. People immediately gravitated towards them, and, within minutes, every hoop was used. People hooped for hours. They cheered each other on and offered support, kindness, and love to each other, all in the spirit of play. The host of the party asked if I'd be open to performing with my hoop for a local show he was putting on. In the spirit of saying yes, I agreed. Weeks later, I performed and from then on began to book hooping gigs, from art shows to children's parties. At one event, a woman approached me about meeting her friend who was doing a documentary on the resurgence of the hula hoop. I met her and told her how I transformed my own mental health and the lives of the students I was working with, in such a short time. The next thing I knew, I was one of the main characters in her documentary, *The Hooping Life.*

THE PRACTICE

THE GET DOWN

Make an Agreement with Yourself to Have Fun

Setting the intention to have fun and play is essential when hooping. You'll face challenges from your inner self (Ego), telling you that you're *doing it wrong* or that your efforts are *not good enough.* This is *not* what play is about. Play is about releasing inhibitions and setting your soul free. Picture yourself as a child at a playground where all you can see is fun. When you notice negative thoughts creeping in that are not in alignment with fun, gently invite them to leave and get back to the mission at hand! No matter your mood put a smile on your face. This action literally **tells** your body that you're happy and having fun. So, invite your inner child to come out and play, and focus on the fun!

Find the Right Hoop

People often tell me they could never hoop, so they stopped trying. My response to this is, "You never had the right hoop!" The hoops you find at a toy store are simply too light and too small for even children to use. Your goal is to find a hoop that is larger in dimension and has some weight to it. All my hula hoops are custom handmade from PVC pipe for a strong and sturdy hoop. For your own custom-made hula hoop that is the perfect size and weight for you, reach out to me directly at www.tishamarina.com.

Play with Different Music Until You Find What Moves You

When I first started hooping with my friend, she loved to hoop to house/techno music. She would jam along and learn new tricks rapidly. I never seemed to find my flow as she did. I Sometimes found myself fighting tears, thinking I wasn't good enough and could never master the art of hooping. Then one night, alone in my living room, I put on my favorite music, hip hop. Suddenly the hoop flowed around my body like magic. It glided with ease, and I found my rhythm. Tricks I could never do immediately came to be, and I felt like a pro! From then on, I became very intentional about what music lit up my soul and then played with my hoop. Let your emotions guide you as to what music to dance to. When I'm feeling sad, I play music that matches my emotions and let the tears fall. When I'm feeling happy, I find upbeat music and let myself rock out. Put on music you'd never imagine hooping to and see what happens. Play with possibilities!

Find the Right Clothing

It's essential to wear clothes that are form-fitting and not too loose when hooping. You don't want the hoop to get caught up in the material as it spins around your body. Be sure to remove all belts and other items from around your waist. Also, clothes too silky can be challenging, as you don't want the hoop to slip around the fabric. For living room hooping, I find my yoga pants and simple t-shirt to be the best option.

Set the Mood and Get Creative

When you hoop, you may find that you go into deep mediation and prayer. Set the space around you to allow for this. Light some candles, burn some incense and set the mood. I often create a small altar of my favorite items, which I place before me to help with my flow. Take a moment to drop into the space and prepare for the magic ahead. Thank the ancestors for the health and the freedom to move your body. Ask them to come down and dance with you. I find that if I'm working through an issue or emotion, that clarity will come to me if I ask for it. I feel it as the hoop spins around my body. I have had many moments of clarity and found solutions to problems by the time my hoop session is over.

Trust the Process

Heads up: your hoop is going to drop to the floor at some point. This is simply called the law of gravity. This drop is not a reflection of how good you are. It may take several times for you to get the hoop to revolve around your waist even once. Just remember to let this process be fun. When the hoop drops, use that moment to your advantage. Bend your knees and let your entire body drop to the ground to pick it up. Know what you just did? You got in a bit of extra exercise and toning for your body and muscles! When the hoop drops, tell yourself, "Great job!" And then pick that beauty back up and **keep going.** Make your determination strong, and remember that you've got this. Be patient with yourself and remember that you're learning something new. This entire exercise is so you can **love yourself up and stay in joy.**

Basic Tips

When someone asks me to teach them how to hoop, I always ask to observe them first. If someone watches how *I* do it, they will try to mimic *me,* which may prevent them from finding their own unique flow and rhythm. Once you start to hoop, your body will guide you. Play with direction. Do you want the hoop to swing to the left or the right? Play with your feet. Put one foot in front of the other, then switch it up and back again. Place both feet side by side. In other words, don't be afraid to experiment, mix it up, and keep the focus on **feeling good.**

Suggestions For Using the Sacred Hoop:

Place the hoop on the lower part of your back, making sure the hoop is even. Don't let the hoop drop too low or go up too high.

Once you have mastered going to the left and the right, switch it up to add some funky dance moves. This is a whole body and mind workout. Use it as such!

Rock back and forth. You might be inclined to move your waist in a circular motion; however, I have found that a rocking back and forth motion (front to back) works best.

This is my own personal story of revolution, and I hope you will use it as an inspiration and launching pad for your own personal transformation. To close out my story, I'd like to share a poem of strength and hope from the Oglala Lakota Sioux. When you choose to embody kindness and compassion within yourself, it has no choice but to ripple out to others. When you change your inner world—and your inner message—you can change the world around you.

Keep on hooping, embody personal kindness, and keep it fun!

I was standing on the highest mountain of them all,
and round about beneath me was the whole hoop of the world.
And while I stood there I saw more than I can tell and I understood more
than I saw;
for I was seeing in a sacred manner the shapes of all things in the spirit,
and the shape of all shapes as they must live together like one being.
And I saw that the sacred hoop of my people was one of many hoops that made
one circle,
wide as daylight and as starlight, and in the center grew one mighty flowering tree
to shelter all children of one mother and one father.
And I saw that it was holy.

Black Elk,
Wichasha Wakan (Medicine Man or Holy Man) of the Oglala Lakota Sioux

Tisha Marina Bernard, MA, is an international speaker and certified peace ambassador. She has worked with thousands of students, schools, and communities, facilitating bully prevention trainings, restorative practices, and trauma-informed counseling circles. She is the founder of I Choose Peace, whose educational mission is to empower young leaders with the courage, compassion, and leadership skills to create peace within themselves and their peers.

Tisha Marina walks the Indigenous/Mexica red road, dedicated to keeping the ancient traditions alive. Her service includes transformative ceremonial healing circles for women, youth, and marginalized communities. Her holistic coaching and therapies are based on the Medicine Wheel and traditional indigenous medicine. Tisha is dedicated to deconstructing and decolonizing emotional wellness and mental health through healing generational trauma and guiding individuals to remember the holistic essence of who they truly are: Divine Creators.

She finds her own inner peace through hoop dance and dancing the ways of the Aztec/Mexica traditions. Through her path as a professional hoop dance performer, she is a featured artist in the popular documentary, The Hooping Life. (www.thehoopinglife.com)

Tisha has a Master's degree in Counseling Psychology and is a licensed Marriage and Family Therapist. She takes a holistic approach towards treating mental health through modalities that include: Somatics, experiential facilitation, psychedelic medicine journeys, and Dialectical Behavioral Therapy.

The cornerstone of all Tisha's work is based in indigenous healing practices, and the transformative power of inclusive dialogue.

For a custom-made hula hoop and/or holistic coaching services, find me at www.tishamarina.com

Connect with Tisha:
Instagram: tisha_sacredhoop
Facebook: Tisha Marina Bernard
LinkedIn: Tisha Marina Bernard

CHAPTER 15

PATRIARCHY-FREE PARENTING

IDENTIFYING SOCIETAL RULES THAT DISEMPOWER YOUR CHILD'S AUTHENTIC SELF-DISCOVERY

Amy M. Wisner, Ph.D.

MY STORY

A message to the people-pleasers, rule followers, and perfectionists: *the more you worry about anyone else's perceptions of you, the more you disempower your child's authentic self-discovery.*

Let me rephrase that with emphasis: the more *you* worry about *anyone* else's perceptions of *you,* the more you *disempower* your beloved child's quest to discover and live into their truest and most authentic self.

Kids learn the *rules of life* by observing everything we say and do.

If you're not outwardly rejecting societal expectations, then you are, by default, perpetuating patriarchy in your child's life.

It's time to reject the rules and start questioning everything.

And I mean, *everything.*

Let me tell you about some rules I learned along the way and how questioning those rules changed my life.

I'll start with a story from 1987. I was an eighth-grader with gravity-defying hair that stayed in place because I used enough Aqua Net to destroy an entire rainforest. My favorite outfits included neon-colored, off-the-shoulder tops with tight-rolled, acid-washed jeans and *two pairs* of layered socks. Not two socks. Two *pairs* of socks.

The layered sock look was somewhat of a signature aesthetic for me. Each morning, I'd color-coordinate my ensemble, carefully layer two pairs of complementary socks, stuff my books into my backpack, and enthusiastically walk to school. Algebra was my first class, and I was always excited to see what we would learn from Mrs. Brown.

One day after class, Mrs. Brown said, "Amy, could you please see me before you leave?"

I immediately thought, *She probably wants to thank me for my enthusiastic participation during class.* I mean, what teacher wouldn't love a straight-A student who is always excited to answer every question they ever ask?

Then, my 13-year-old mind started racing.

Oh no! What if she wants me to stop raising my hand? Maybe she's annoyed that I never give anyone else a chance to answer. My first-grade teacher always told me that I raised my hand too much. Shit. I feel so stupid. I should have acted like I didn't know the answers. Why do I always have to be such a know-it-all?

I slid my backpack straps onto my shoulders and nervously cinched them too tight, then reluctantly approached Mrs. Brown. Her curly hair was wildly unkempt, and her glasses were a bit too large for her face. Until this moment, I'd never really noticed that she didn't wear makeup.

She said, "Amy, thank you for staying. I wanted to tell you that I love your willingness to express yourself with your clothes. I overheard Jim teasing you about your socks, but I personally think the coordinating socks are a nice touch."

I felt the embarrassment spreading from the pit of my stomach to my suddenly bright red cheeks.

She exclaimed, "Don't be embarrassed! Be proud of yourself for having the courage to be yourself. Please don't ever lose that."

Feigning confidence and begging my face to return to its normal color, I forced a smile and said, "Okay, I'll try not to."

She encouragingly continued, "I don't think you realize how rare it is for people to just be themselves. I see how bold you are when answering questions in class, yet recently you seem concerned about what other people think. Don't let them dissuade you from living your truth."

My thoughts raced again.

How did she know I was worried about what other people thought? Is it that obvious I'm thinking about the jerk boys in class calling me a brown-nosing teacher's pet? And what in the world does "living your truth" even mean?

I thanked her and left the classroom as quickly as possible.

As I walked down the hallway toward my locker, something felt different inside. I was suddenly self-conscious about my entire outfit. My mind started racing again.

Why was Jim such a jerk? Why did he have to make fun of me loud enough for Mrs. Brown to hear it? Why do I wear these stupid socks anyway? From this point forward, I need to wear one pair of socks and stop answering so many questions in class. I'll just keep my know-it-all mouth shut.

My thoughts preoccupied me as I rifled through my locker, looking for my Bonnie Bell lip gloss. *I wonder why Mrs. Brown doesn't wear makeup. That's kind of weird.* The bell rang as I finished applying the cherry-scented shimmer to my lips. My thoughts shifted to a hopeful giddiness; *I hope I see Andy on my way to class. I know how much he loves this lip gloss.*

Over the next several years, my awareness of others' opinions continued to dominate my thoughts. Boldness and creativity were replaced with cautiousness and conformity. I paid close attention to people's opinions and tailored my behavior accordingly. I listened to the way girls talked about other girls, the way boys talked about girls, and the way adults talked about girls and women. I was a people-pleaser, after all. I surely wanted to know what people believed a young woman *should* be.

As it turns out, a great way to learn what someone *believes* is to listen to what they *say* about people. Sexist jokes, snide comments, and hushed gossip about strangers and acquaintances were incredibly informative about the *rules of life*. But some of the most meaningful information I gathered was from observing the way women around me harshly judged themselves and constrained themselves to the rules.

I made mental notes about everything to avoid. *Don't be loud. Don't be opinionated. Don't be fat. Don't be too skinny. Don't complain. Don't be too positive. Don't wear too much makeup. Don't go without makeup. Don't let your gray hair show. And most importantly, do not be a know-it-all and don't be bossy.*

This growing mental list of rules was surely something I could live up to. You see, for the better part of my life, I was a card-carrying member of the Good Girl Club. I followed the rules, always did my homework, got good grades, and *certainly* never got in trouble. This new list of rules for being the perfect girl had met its match. I was ready to put that list into action.

I stopped raising my hand in class, especially if one of the boys had his hand raised. I started wearing more subdued clothing and *absolutely* stopped wearing those stupid socks. I bought *Teen Magazine* so I could learn the hot trends and understand what boys liked in a girl.

I remained steadfast in my efforts to be less bossy and less opinionated, especially with boys. If a boy said something inaccurate or illogical, I'd politely discuss it in a way that wouldn't fracture his delicate ego. With time, I realized it was easier and more pleasing to others if I happily nodded my head in agreement. I was leveling myself up to the societal standard of being the right kind of girl.

The strangest thing happened, though. The more I tried to become the perfect girl, the more validation I needed from the world around me. The more I became what I figured everyone else wanted from me, the less I felt any sense of worthiness.

I'd transformed myself into a perfectly polite, less opinionated, and much more subtle version of myself. But I needed near-constant reassurance that I was doing it right. Apparently, that bold girl inside me, who Mrs. Brown cautioned me to never lose, had been traded in for a much less authentic and more insecure version of myself. This new version of me was terrified of getting it wrong.

Fast forward to the summer of 2012. Twenty years had passed since I'd graduated from high school. My hair spray usage had plummeted, and my penchant for anything neon or acid-washed was a distant memory. I'd been married and divorced *twice* and lived in North Carolina, Colorado, California, and Hawaii before coming full circle back to Michigan for my Ph.D. program at Michigan State.

While completing my doctoral studies, I worked full time as an account executive for a laboratory that runs infectious disease testing for transplant patients. My territory covered all major hospitals in the upper Midwest from the Dakotas to Michigan. I spent every week flying on planes, living in hotels, and meeting with doctors, nurses, and lab directors all week until returning home to Michigan on Friday nights. I spent Saturdays recuperating and doing laundry. Then on Sundays, I prepared for the week and packed my bag to do it all over again.

This kind of work travel was new for me. I'd never been away from home nearly this much. It was fun spending time in cities like Chicago, Milwaukee, Minneapolis, and Fargo (not kidding, Fargo is great!), but I was exhausted. I made every effort to avoid weekend plans that required leaving my apartment or wearing pants.

The biggest barrier to meeting my *pants-less weekend* goal was my time-consuming hair coloring routine. You see, I found my first gray hair at 22 years old and *immediately* started dying my whole head of hair. God forbid somebody would see my gray hair and think I was old! *The audacity.*

At this point in my life, I'd been coloring my gray hair for 16 years. This beauty ritual initially took place every 6-8 weeks, but as more of my hair turned gray, my salon visits became more frequent. The combination of regular salon visits and my demanding travel schedule was about to result in a moment of reckoning.

One sunny Saturday morning, I was sprawled out on my oversized orange chair with a large mug of freshly brewed coffee in one hand and my phone in the other. Tucker, my deaf, white chihuahua, was happily napping on my lap for the first time since the previous Saturday. My work travel was definitely getting in the way of our cuddle time. As I mindlessly scrolled through pictures on my phone and sipped coffee, I received a reminder notification, *Hair Appointment with Kailey in 30 minutes.*

Well, shit! I totally forgot about that, I thought. *There goes three hours of my day. Didn't I just get my hair colored?*

I scrolled back through my calendar. *Three weeks ago? I just had my hair colored three weeks ago? How do I already have this much gray showing? Goddamn it.*

I sat my phone and coffee down, scooped Tucker into my arms, snuggled him up to my face, and said, "I'm so sorry, buddy. I've gotta get my hair colored. We wouldn't want people to think I'm old! Right?" He sighed a deep sigh of resignation as I begrudgingly placed him in his fluffy bed.

As I pulled on a pair of jeans, I paused.

Wait.

Why the fuck do I even care if people think I'm old?

Pulling a beige sweater over my head, I paused again.

Why does my age even matter? Who fucking cares how old I am? Why are we all so obsessed with never seeming old? Where did that even come from?

I walked across the hallway from my bedroom to the small bathroom and took a long, hard look in the mirror.

Why have I never questioned this? Why have I been operating as if it is a fact of life that a woman with gray hair must cover it up with dye?

Dad has a whole head of white hair, and he's never even mentioned the thought of coloring it. Hell, he's the reason I have this hair.

I stood back, imagined myself with his hair, then chuckled aloud. His standard response if someone says we look alike is, "You should see her with white hair." Hardy, har, har. *Oh, Dad jokes.*

I walked to the living room, grabbed my phone, and gave Tucker a big kiss on the head. I nuzzled my face in his tiny neck and said, "You know what, little man. I'm gonna quit this shit. You and I can rock white hair together!"

I went to that appointment and asked Kailey to bleach the shit out of my hair. I told her I was letting my gray grow out. As evidenced by the gape of her mouth, she was mortified. Once she recovered from the shock, she said, "I've heard this from clients before. Trust me. You'll be back in here for full-color as soon as you see what's under there." I thought, *geez, dude, thanks for the moral support.*

As anyone who knows me can tell you, the best way to get me to do anything with gusto is to tell me it's not possible. I took this new challenge *head-on* (pun absolutely intended.)

Here's the thing, once I peeked behind the curtain and realized the Wizard was just some old, cranky dude with a microphone, I started questioning everything. And I mean *everything.*

All those rules I learned as a girl; were just societal norms. I started asking myself who benefited from these norms. The obvious answers were the multi-billion-dollar beauty, health and fitness, and weight loss industries. But I knew there was more to it.

As I questioned my beliefs about the *rules of life,* my identity shifted. Ditching the hair dye was one very liberating step outside societal expectations. Only a few years later, I made the boldest, bravest, and most liberating decision of my life when I became a single mom by choice via double-donor IVF.

The day my daughter, Olivia, entered the world, the fiercest version of me was also born. This version of me was the grown-up, fuck-all-y'all's-opinions version of that bold and expressive little girl Mrs. Brown told me to hold onto. She was back, she was older and wiser, and she was not taking shit from anyone.

That, my friend, is who's writing to you today. I am a social justice warrior on a mission to dismantle systems of oppression one self-loving, authentic, kind, and compassionate act at a time. What I've realized is that the most insidious tool of patriarchy is the hustle for external validation. As parents, we are our children's first line of defense against the persistent messaging about what a *good girl* or a *real man* looks like.

Every child is born with a uniquely wild spirit. Kids are creative geniuses with endless curiosity. They are innate learners who love adventure, exploration and learning just for the fun of it. They watch everything we do and hear everything we say. Unfortunately, a lot of what we do and say is a function of our own patriarchal conditioning.

If we want to raise children who are confident in their beautiful, wild selves and are not victims of patriarchy's toxic messages of *never enough,* then we must become aware of our own indoctrination. Our self-discovery is the beginning of the resistance. Rejecting patriarchal rules is how we halt the generational passing of its oppressive torch.

THE PRACTICE

I've created a questionnaire to assess the ways you may be unintentionally disempowering your child's authentic self-discovery through your own thoughts and behaviors. Please fight your inclination to answer in a socially desirable way. As you read the questions, you will have a sense of why I'm asking them. Do your absolute best to answer honestly and objectively. Over-scoring yourself serves no purpose. Patriarchy is in us all. Honest self-assessment is key to growth.

For each question, jot down your score (1-5) for each prompt, then add all ten scores together. Refer to the guide below for your results.

Score according to the following scale:

> 1 = never
>
> 2 = not often
>
> 3 = sometimes
>
> 4 = often
>
> 5 = always

How often do you. . .

1. Get angry with yourself for doing something stupid?
2. Chastise yourself for making a mistake?
3. Worry about being photographed because of your appearance?
4. Struggle to choose clothing because you're worried about how you look?
5. Look in the mirror and notice your flaws (e.g., wrinkles, under-eye circles, dry skin, sagging bits?)
6. Feverishly clean and organize before someone comes over?
7. Worry what someone will think about your parenting choices?

8. Worry about what someone will think about your child's behavior?

9. Say something mean to yourself that you wouldn't say to someone else?

10. Hesitate to share your thoughts because of what people may think?

Total your score and refer to the guide below.

Ten or less: Rebel from Birth

Where the hell did you even grow up? Please, teach me your ways. Coffee's on me.

11-20: Rebel in Action

Keep fighting the good fight by loving yourself and telling everyone to fuck right off. Can we be friends?

21-30: Rebel-ish

You're obviously doing some good work to fight patriarchy's stronghold. I'm here for you if you want to get soul-aligned. Maybe we can invite some Rebel from Birth folks to help!

31+: Rebel to Be

Patriarchy has you by the neck, but I'm here for you. I was in your shoes until I started questioning everything. I still fight against those pervasive thoughts, but I do so with mindfulness. Let's connect.

The kindest thing we can do for our children is model the resistance by living into our most authentic versions of ourselves. If we want to raise kids who truly **know themselves, deeply love themselves,** and reject society's bullshit expectations, we need to model that behavior for them. We must discover our souls and learn to genuinely love ourselves.

Let me help you discover who you are at the core of your being, what you truly care about, and how to reject patriarchal expectations so you can be your most authentic self. This transformation takes vigilance and hard work, and you'll need support. Come on over to the rebellion to find your people. We've got t-shirts.

To schedule a self-discovery call, visit: www.cancelthepatriarchy.org.

While you're there, grab my Rebel's Recommended Reading list so you can start your rebel journey today.

Amy M. Wisner, Ph.D., is audacious and unapologetic in her quest to dismantle oppressive systems by helping people become their most authentic selves. As a former rule-following good girl, she can deeply empathize with anyone who struggles to break the rules. Once upon a time, she wanted nothing more than to check the patriarchal life boxes, keep everyone happy, and live happily ever after.

After powering through the not-so-happily-ever-after, Amy chose a different path. At nearly 40 years old, she began a rebel journey of questioning the rules and discovering her truth within. Amy stopped coloring her gray hair, became a single mom by choice through double-donor IVF, and got a bunch of tattoos. She's now living her best life as Olivia and Caleb's mom, a professor at Michigan State University, and the founder of The Rebellion @cancelthepatriarchy.org.

Amy is an interpersonal communication researcher, professor, and lifelong learner with a background in business and a deep need to understand human communication behavior. She researches social influence with the goal of identifying the kinds of people who can create meaningful social change.

Amy recently launched the RebelED 1BIG Coaching program aimed at helping dreamers become achievers through self-discovery, value-alignment, and intense focus on one bold, inspired goal (1BIG). This coaching program was designed for people who have a million great ideas but struggle to focus and finish strong.

To learn more about Amy's rebel journey, check out her TEDxMSU talk. She discusses how patriarchy is disadvantaging women and men. She also shares her story of becoming a single mom by choice. Join The Rebellion and start smashing the patriarchy one self-loving, authentic, kind, and compassionate act at a time.

Connect with Amy:

Website: www.cancelthepatriarchy.org

Social media: https://linktr.ee/cancelthepatriarchy

CHAPTER 16

THE DIAMOND RULE

SPEAK TO YOURSELF AS YOU WOULD TO SOMEONE YOU LOVE

Blake Zealear, Relationship Engineer

MY STORY

"I suck," he muttered to himself as he stared blankly at the monitor.

"Why is this so fucking hard for me?"

His mind raced through nightmare scenarios of failure and ridicule. He chewed on his fingernails as he imagined all the awful ways he'd feel if he tried to set up a business and then made a mistake.

You're going to crash and burn, just like your father, he thought.

He closed the laptop with a swipe of rejection and got up from the desk to smoke another cigarette. The tobacco brought only minor relief to his word-laden mind.

This is what always happens. I can't get ahead if I can't get out of my head. He cursed, "what is *wrong with me?!*"

He resigned himself to another day of doing only low-risk tasks and putting off the bigger challenges of creating his dreams, perhaps until the day when he was no longer mired in a swamp of disempowerment. But when would that day come? History would suggest—and his brain would remind him—*fucking never.*

A short time later, his beloved came home from work which was a welcome distraction from the solitary hell of attempting self-employment.

"How was your day, sweetie?" he asked.

"It was awful. I'm so tired of commuting, and Steve hardly even notices all the work I'm doing for him. He's constantly in meetings, and we haven't had our usual chats in like two weeks. Every day is the same, and the people at the office are like tech zombies. We have nothing in common."

"Babe, you could totally ask for a new role or just quit. Any company would be stoked to have you on their team."

"You think so?" she asked skeptically. "I'm so scared of not having a paycheck."

"I get it, and you have lots of options! I bet if you started looking for an alternative, you'd find that you're way less stuck than you think."

"Yeah, you're probably right. I could try talking to Steve and telling him I'm not super happy with this role. Maybe he'll have an idea of where I might be a better fit. If nothing comes of that, then at least I still have a job!"

"Absolutely! I'll help you dust off your resume if you want to start applying elsewhere, too."

"Aw, thanks, babe! You're the best cheerleader!"

The contrast in these two scenes exemplifies one of the greatest failures of kindness that plague people's lives. Many of us simply do not treat ourselves the way we treat others.

We live in violation of The Diamond Rule, the overlooked corollary of the Golden Rule. We don't hold ourselves as precious.

The Golden Rule we learned as children is as enduring in our memory as the Pledge of Allegiance: "Do unto others as you would have them do unto you." But its converse: "Do unto *yourself* as you would do unto others," is conspicuously absent from our social conditioning. Why is that?

Frankly, I attribute this to millennia of religious dogma. The Second Commandment, for example, "Thou shall not make thyself an idol," was likely intended to dissuade people from believing they are God(s). Then generations of clergy regurgitated it to reinforce the value of humility: "Don't say anything *too* nice about yourself," but most people adapted it to "don't say *anything* nice about yourself." Over time, countless kind-hearted people were taught not to speak kindly of themselves.

Herein lies a problem, however, because your words create your world.

At the intersection of psychology and transformational growth, there is a modality called Neuro-Linguistic Programming (NLP). As the name suggests, NLP looks at the power of language to program, and reprogram, your mind. It holds that your mind does not accurately represent reality, it interprets reality like a map interprets a landscape. This means no one is living in a truly objective reality.

We are all living in a frame of reference shaped, colored, and textured by our minds, specifically by the words we say and *think*.

Contrary to popular belief, our words and thoughts determine how we see and feel things, rather than the way things look determines how we think and feel. Most of us move through life feeling like outside circumstances or past events have the absolute power to shape our reality. As you will see, this is simply not the case. *You* have the power to shape your reality.

The words we employ can create a feedback loop of disempowerment with the potential to derail anyone from going after what they want.

When you have a harsh thought like, *I suck,* your brain releases neuropeptides that hit your emotional centers painfully, sending signals back to your brain that you are upset, which makes your thoughts harsher, leading to, *I may as well give up.*

It's a spell you're under, cast unknowingly by your well-meaning but unconscious mind trying to use criticism and blame to light a fire under your ass. It's not a terribly effective strategy, though, burning yourself up with words. Such a spell usually just leaves you with a burnt ass that can't sit comfortably anywhere.

Being *unaware* of this aspect of having a mind is maddening. It's as if the critical voices in our heads are sadistic torturers, relentless in their punishment. If they would only shut up for a moment, you might be able to summon courage, feel inspired, or motivate yourself to try something new. But no—the tyranny of words, thoughts, and feelings that cascade through our untrained minds are the master, and the master will not be pacified, at least not with the thinking that got you into this mess.

Whatever it is you want in life that you're also afraid of—money, love, sex, more power, greater expression—all of it is on the other side of a loving, powerful, honest, vulnerable conversation with yourself. Or, more accurately, your *selves*.

With patience, some well-held boundaries, and The Diamond Rule, you can transform your life by speaking to yourself, and the characters inside you, with profound kindness. The best part is, you probably already know how to do it and do it well. It's really quite simple: speak to your selves just like you would speak to your best friend, beloved, or child (many of them are your inner children, after all.)

When we speak to those we love, we most often come from compassion, encouragement, generosity, sweetness, and possibility. We remind our loved ones how loved they are. We praise their glowing qualities and forgive them for their shortcomings. We see them as full of potential rather than limited by circumstance. We make light of their idiosyncrasies and celebrate their uniqueness. We give them the benefit of the doubt, and we express delight! In other words, we speak to them with words of affirmation, employing an entire language of love that has the power to quell fear, open hearts, and inspire greatness.

Why then do we reserve all of this kindness and empowering language for others? Why don't we simply turn inward and duplicate the same acts of love with ourselves? When I have asked this question to so many loved ones and clients, I usually get the same response: "Because I don't deserve it."

Another spell cast by another sentence of imprisonment.

Like most people, if you go back in your memory, you can probably find evidence of why you deserve to suffer. This is confirmation bias of a belief that you already held, however. Confirmation bias is a "bug" of the human mind that sorts for information that agrees with what we already believe and discards that which disagrees. Why evolution didn't eliminate this by now makes no sense to me, but here we are.

So, it's almost impossible to find the inception of a belief like; *I deserve to suffer.* It occurred so long ago that the chicken-or-egg question about whether you deserve all the good things in life or you have earned your misery has no clear beginning. *Was any of that evidence real, or just my mind stuck on an interpretation?*

Posing the mere question of whether or not you deserve to be kind to yourself is *itself* casting a spell! By asking this, you're implying that the decision is still in deliberation, which is perhaps another religious relic, like Judgment Day. As if there is any *real* question about your innate goodness or lovability!

Do you ever really ask such a question of ultimate judgment about those you love?! Of course not. You've outgrown these old-fashioned ideas of good and bad, right and wrong, at least in the way you treat others. You might not like what they do, but you wouldn't sentence them to eternal damnation. If anything, you have a confirmation bias that they still deserve to be happy, loved, and safe, regardless of their sins.

This discrepancy is the definition of a double standard, and it is the major violation of The Diamond Rule. *Other people get the Diamond treatment, but not me.*

So what are we to do? All of these unanswerable questions, biases of the mind, eons of moralistic programming, spells upon spells, all conspiring to create a world that keeps us living uncomfortably inside of our comfort zones!? It's enough to make you want to give up, just as I wanted to give up before I smashed through the walls of language that imprisoned me and became the self-made person I am today.

The man in the opening story, perhaps obviously, was me. The revelation that set me free is what I'm here to share with you.

If you speak and think your words with the same love and care that you'd use with someone you truly love, everything changes.

Your beliefs become malleable, then nothing, then open to creation.

You discover that you are actually a magician, casting spells with every breath.

You will feel yourself as the creator of your reality instead of a pawn in a greater reality.

Eventually, you will come to see that you actually are the greatest love of your life.

And when you embrace that truth, you will be *unstoppable.*

The practice that follows will teach you how to use words and thoughts with kindness and nurturance. It requires patience, openness, precision, discipline, sweetness, cunning, and courage, but don't let that scare you!

Even the smallest gesture of self-kindness will start the spiral turning in the right direction. Over time, you will become so adept at treating yourself like the diamond you are that you'll wonder how you ever did differently!

THE PRACTICE

THE DIAMOND RULE PRACTICE

Step 1: Listen

Begin by paying mindful attention to your thoughts, the words you say, and the voices inside your head. Get a journal and start to make notes of the scripts that are already running. You may need to sit quietly in meditation with the willingness to hear them to clearly discern what is being said. At this starting place, however, simply observe the scripts as you listen. Don't accept the stories about yourself as facts.

Step 2: Get Curious and Talk with Your Selves

Each of us has many sub-personalities, or *selves,* that comprise our greater personality. The looping thoughts and feelings we get stuck in can be viewed as one or more of your selves being noisy and clamoring for attention. So, give them attention! Engage with each voice like you were meeting someone new, and start a loving conversation with them. Have a dialogue out loud with each sub-self, where you embody both that voice and an inner facilitator. You can refer to your whole self by name in the third person and even switch seats to represent both sides of the conversation.

It might go something like this:

Inner Facilitator (F): "Hey there, it seems you have some important things to say, and I'd like to understand you better. Can we talk?"

Inner Critic (C): "Sure, but I'm not very happy right now."

F: "That's okay. Maybe I can help you feel better as we talk. Can you tell me a little about yourself? What is your role in Blake's life?"

C: "Well, I'm here to make sure he doesn't fuck up, to keep him out of trouble, and prevent him from being a failure."

F: "That sounds like important work. Thanks for doing it! How do you go about doing your job?"

C: "Well, I criticize him and make him feel bad about himself, so he doesn't take stupid risks."

F: "And how's that going for you two? Do you feel good about your relationship?"

C: "Not really. He resents me, and he's scared of me. He wishes I would just shut up and die."

F: "Well, killing you isn't an option; you're too important! Perhaps we can work out a different strategy for you to help Blake. One that builds gratitude instead of resentment. Are you open to that?"

C: "If it would get me out of the dog-house and help him out, sure. I'm open to that."

F: "Thank you for your willingness. I imagine a new role for you as Director of Encouragement. Instead of using criticism and ridicule to motivate Blake, how about using encouragement, affirmation, and levity to help him stay out of trouble. Do you think you can do that?"

C: "Director of Encouragement, huh? I like the sound of that! Okay, yes! I can try being kinder and seeing how that works."

F: "Thank you for this conversation. I'm so glad we talked!"

This is a somewhat abbreviated example, and I encourage you to expand your conversations with this tone and structure.

The keys to engaging with your inner selves are similar to speaking with an upset child, friend, or loved one.

Remember to:

- Be curious and open.
- Ask consent to get more intimate.
- Assume the best intentions.
- Witness without judgment.
- Express gratitude.
- Aim for cooperation rather than conflict.
- Upgrade the sub-self's reality to one that suits it and you better.

Keep in mind that all the disempowering selves inside you are actually trying to protect you from repeating the pain of the past. They were born in response to trauma, and they are derived from cross-sections of parents, authority figures, friends and siblings, and societal dictums of good and bad. They are not evil; they are parts of you that have been misled into using abuse rather than love as a vehicle for action. All of them just want to be loved, heard, and understood. Once they are, they usually become quiet and cooperative. Then they will help you write new scripts that change the game.

Some of your selves may need to be downright stood up to, like a playground bully. You may have to draw clear boundaries against their behavior, but you do so as an act of love for the greater whole. Identifying the selves' strengths and rewriting their job description to put their talents in service of peace and harmony is the goal. A bully can make an excellent boundary enforcer, for example. No self left behind or even demoted.

It is helpful to visualize all your parts as members of a commission, knights of a round table, or passengers on the plane that is flying in the direction of your expansion. With each conversation, you can gain buy-in from each member. Eventually, they will align with the greater mission of your wholeness and well-being.

Step 3: Develop Countering Affirmations

For each disempowering message you hear, develop a new script for that self to use. For example, if the old script said, "I'll never get the love I want," try using something like, "The love I want is just around the corner." This will likely feel awkward at first because it is running counter to *decades* of the old script.

The key here is to fake it 'til you make it. Use the new scripts again and again. Say them in a mirror. Repeat them with increasing sincerity until you start to believe them. You'll know it's working when the words start to land in your body with pleasure and relief. It may even make you cry the first dozen or so times you sincerely say to yourself, "I love you, [Name]. You are a wonderful person."

The more you repeat these affirmations to yourself, the more you will believe them, and the more your confirmation bias will sort for evidence that they are true. The "bug" becomes a feature. Now you are using NLP kindness spell-casting to generate an upward spiral of reinforcing love messages.

Step 4: Take it Even Deeper into All-out Romance

Listen to the words you say to your partner or would say to the love of your life. Then turn that mushy, gooey goodness on yourself! Try calling yourself sweetheart, baby, my love, darling, etc. Flatter yourself, pay yourself compliments. Pull out all the stops! This isn't narcissism, it's soul integration!

Look yourself in the mirror and give yourself the gaze of adoration that you usually only reserve for that special someone. Treat yourself like the human of your dreams and nothing less. Because you've known deep down all along that you fucking deserve it! In time, your reality will come to match your words.

Step 5: Bring Discipline to the Practice

Keep sharpening your language-blade, and stay vigilant for any disempowering messages sneaking through. Once the loudest selves have been addressed, the subtler and quieter ones will surface to be heard and loved.

When you say something like, "Why can't I figure this out?" softly tell yourself, "Hey, that's not helping, my love." How about, "You're smart, you'll figure it out!"

Keep listening and playing with word choices, and be compassionate with yourself if this feels uncomfortable for a while. You *are* doing it right!

If you address all your selves and love them all, your mind will eventually become a profoundly quiet place. Then it becomes much easier to manifest your goals because you can *actually hear* your heart, desires, and dreams.

Once you can hear *those* selves, give them a voice, too! Declare your truth and your brilliance to the world! Use your words, the mirror, and supportive people in your life as amplifiers for your practice. Speak your new truth to them and absorb their responses!

Soon, the spiky, cold inner landscape you were used to will give way to a plush, warm, and inviting refuge.

You are becoming the master of your own mind. You are embracing the love of your life. You are living by the Diamond Rule.

Welcome home, my love.

Blake is a relationship engineer, revolutionary author, and transformational guide, working with individuals, couples, and groups to create the love and lives of their dreams. Blake is also a practitioner and facilitator of Sacred Sexuality, trained at the International School of Temple Arts (ISTA). His passion is contributing to the expansion of others to discover their truth, power, and purpose. His devotion is to growing the Collective for planetary transformation.

Blake can be reached through his website: www.blakezealear.com, where you can book a session or sign up for his mailing list for access to future events.

CHAPTER 17

WRITING YOUR FUTURE

THE GIFT OF UNEXPECTED EVENTS

Tina Muheim, Executive Leadership and Life Coach

MY STORY

Have you ever had a moment when you knew your life was about to change—a moment you dreaded but couldn't stop? I can still recall and feel all the feelings waiting to hear my fate. My organization had yet another IT reorganization planned. There was one about every six months. *Here we go again!* The talk around the organization was that the next reorganization would be different, and the structure of the IT department would also be different.

The day came in November 2019 when management scheduled to meet with IT associates to determine whether we would continue with the company. I had the longest tenure within my company's IT department. There was a buzz in the air where you could feel something was about to change, and my emotions were running high. *What will happen to me? Would they even think of letting me go? I understood the business, and people liked me; why am I worrying? Okay, but if they let me go, I'll be okay. Think of the time off you could have. Tina, isn't that what you've wanted over the years? Isn't that what you've been saying—if they want you to leave, they will have to make you go?* Other departments were also waiting to hear the news and how the changes would impact them.

I joined my company straight out of college. It was exciting to be working at an *adult* job. After a few years in the telemarketing department (*there were six of us, does six make a department?*), I received a promotion into the IT department, where I found new friends and learned a lot. I was in my element. My jam was the excitement of going to work, fixing problems, and helping other departments figure out the best ways of doing things. I had fantastic managers who taught me about technology and leadership. It was family. There were times when I hated Fridays because I didn't want to leave work. *Crazy, right?* I loved my job and the satisfaction it gave me. It was easy for me to work weekends and late evenings. I was happy to help and serve those I was working with and the other departments. I knew the work we provided helped them do their jobs better. And at the end of the day, the IT work helped make money for the company. I wanted all of us to be successful.

On that fateful day in November, my spidey sense told me something big was about to happen. I'm not a fan of rollercoasters, yet my stomach was on a ride. My feelings were all over the place, waiting to hear whether they were staying or going. *Oh, to be a fly on the wall.* Everyone returning had good news, except for a new reporting structure which was nothing earth-shattering. I was calm, then nervous. I'm an emotional eater, so I'm sure that day I was looking for comfort food in the vending machines— Oreo cookies and Swedish Fish—come to mind. Just one more cookie fish sandwich! Food of champions when the going gets tough!

I was the last to get called into the room. I don't recall someone from the room calling me into the room. I remember the last person telling me I was next, "Tina, you're next. Don't worry; everything will be fine." *Easy for them to say. Keep breathing. Keep it all together. You got this! Maybe that last cookie fish sandwich was not a good idea.* My body was warm, the tingling coming up my body with a tightness in my chest and throat. I kept breathing, trying to stay calm. There were three people in the room and someone on the phone. As they started all the formal talk, I thought, *just get to the point.* My spidey sense kept saying, *you're out, and when they say it, don't react. Don't let them see you upset.* Finally, the teacher's voice from Charlie Brown stopped, and I heard, "And for you to receive your severance, you need to stay until the end of February 2020." I smiled and thanked them as all my insides were trying to keep it together.

I did break down once I was alone. The decision to let me go shocked many of my coworkers. I had four months before leaving, so in my mind, there was a chance this would all work out, and I wouldn't be going. During those last four months, it was a slow death—the process of grieving for the only work life I knew. *Did you know grief comes in different forms, and its stages don't always appear in any natural order?* Reality hit when I realized I needed to update my resume. I laughed; my last resume was 33 years old. Yeah, it was hard knowing I had to look for another job. *What were the positions available to me? Who will hire me at 55 years old? Am I too old to be hired? How many more years could I work at another job after working 33 years for the same company?* I know it's unheard of for people to stay at one company for so long, but my company was family with many of us growing up there.

I did all the things—resume writing, cover letters, networking. Networking was not something I enjoyed (*actually, I hated it*), but I pressed forward with it because it's how you find a new job. At least it's what everyone told me. I even applied to other positions inside the company. However, there was an expectation of moving to the corporate location, and I wasn't interested in moving out of state. I couldn't understand why moving to the corporate location was critical when we had people working remotely.

The last week of February 2020 arrived. Throughout the months, I prepared, throwing things out, organizing digital folders of all the information others needed from me, and working to find a new job. *It's exhausting trying to brain dump 33 years of information and look for a new job.* I made a spontaneous decision to go back to school since I'd have time on my hands as I looked for a job. I enrolled in a Doctor of Information Technology program to keep me busy. *Yes, what was I thinking?* Keeping busy was my way of coping and avoiding the feelings of grief, sadness, anger, and worry. Whatever came up, I pushed down.

On my last day, I did cry, and the hardest was saying goodbye to a dear friend. "I'll miss our talks," I said. "Stop worrying; we'll still talk. Your friendship means the world to me, and I won't forget you," they said. *The words left me bawling like a baby.* In my mind, I would never see them again, and my heart ached with sadness, rejection, and abandonment. The first weekend home was a blur. It was like every other weekend, except I had the boxes sitting in front of me from work. I was on a mission: start school and find a job. *I'll prove to everyone that I'm a survivor.* School started and quickly brought me into my comfort zone of learning. It excited me to be studying at coffee shops, lunching with friends for my upcoming birthday, and waking up on my schedule. No more alarm clocks.

I never made it to a coffee shop. I never had any birthday lunches. I did get to experience waking up on my schedule. And, I would have never predicted that everything would shut down for a month and a half within two weeks of leaving for a pandemic. Well, as we know, six weeks stretched longer and longer. I was a high risk for mental health issues—living alone, recently let go from my job, and now a pandemic that removed human contact from me. The perfect storm made for the ideal space for two things to happen to me—decide what I wanted to do when I grew up or crack under pressure. I might splinter, but I never break.

By May 2020, I realized I didn't want to go back to corporate unless I could make an impact. The years of being a worker bee were over. The flip-flopping of my stomach when I looked at and submitted job postings was enough of a sign that I was going in the wrong direction. I learned I had a choice. I was allowed to choose my path and build the life I desired. Along with school, I enrolled in a transformational coaching program to help me be my most authentic self.

I like helping people. It makes me happy to see that I can make a difference in someone's life. I struggled with depression, not being good enough, and never seeing my value, yet I'm an over-achiever and people-pleaser. I should have all the things. I don't. Everything is easy when I am my authentic being. Relationships are easy, schoolwork is easy, and finding my bliss is easy. Being me is easy.

I started a new career as a coach while still going to school. I've mainly stayed isolated, except for Zoom calls and an occasional in-person lunch. And I've been the happiest I've been in a long time. *How can this be?* I learned a lot about myself over the last two years. I didn't understand "putting your oxygen mask on first before helping others" until I started to carve out what I wanted in life. I discovered a determination and resiliency I knew I had but didn't previously see those strengths. I learned I could do more for myself by putting myself first and learning to say no. I learned that it's okay to go slow and get a vision of what I want. I realized that I'm good enough and bring value to everyone I meet. I learned that "done, not perfect" is okay.

I'm grateful for the pandemic and for leaving my job after 33 years of service. It's okay to fear change. Change provides motions like the waves in the ocean. Change provides us with opportunities that we may never have gotten before. Change allows us to reinvent ourselves. I reinvented myself and did so every day. I have no plan B, so I move forward in building a new career as a coach, helping others on the verge of burnout, and feeling like there's no way out. I was that person, and there is a way out, but it may not mean leaving your job.

Finding a new path in a career also brought me to love myself more. Even though all the schoolwork and chaos may be floating around me, I love my life. I am not the same person who walked out of work on February 28, 2020, thinking the impossible. I'm an amazing badass and have authenticity, power, heart, charisma, and source. I'm grateful to the universe for giving me the kick I needed to know I am here to do more. What more are you here to do? What changes can you make today that will give you a different tomorrow?

THE PRACTICE

Take out your journal or piece of paper and a pen.

1. Write down one or two changes you'd like to make or see differently in your life.

2. Look at these changes and ask yourself: *How will my life be different if I make these one or two changes? What differences will these changes make in reinventing myself?*

3. Now imagine your life one year from today. *What are you doing? What does the day feel like when you wake up?* See and feel what you're experiencing. Close your eyes to see the colors and textures around you, listen to the sounds, smell the smells, and get all your senses involved.

4. Write a letter from your future self letting yourself know all that is possible from the one or two changes you'll make starting today. Don't forget to date the letter one year from today.

5. Read the letter every day as a reminder that everything you want is inside you.

6. One year from today, celebrate the changes you've made and the life you created for yourself.

Tina Muheim is an executive leadership and life coach. She works with people in tech who are succeeding and on the verge of burnout. They want to figure out if there's a way to manage their careers differently to stay healthy and have a life outside of work. Tina has 33 years of insurance and technology experience and is pursuing her Doctor of Information Technology degree. She is EQi 2.0/360 certified, trauma and DEI informed, and a volunteer crisis counselor, allowing her to create a safe place for clients to make transformational changes.

Connect with Tina:

LinkedIn: www.linkedin.com/in/tinamuheim

Website: tinamuheim.com

CHAPTER 18

THE PRESCRIPTION FOR KINDNESS

KILLING CONDITIONED NICENESS IN MEDICINE

Dr. Lisa Tharler, Mentor and Coach for Frontline Physicians, CEO and Founder of Under the White Coat MD

MY STORY

In this real-life kink scene, my cheeks are turning flush. I remember the feel of leather and the riding crop in my hand and how its playful sting left lingering redness on my partner's skin. I mounted him, knowing he was blindfolded and didn't have permission to reply to my humiliating taunts:

"You're worthless. You're pathetic. I could only be riding you out of pity. I feel so sorry for you. You'd better not come. Yes!"

"Amazing scene," yells my coach.

Oh my goodness, how did I end up here?

My journey of healing and integration has certainly taken me to some very interesting places.

As a composed doctor, compassionate wife, and responsible mother of three, I frequently hide my human judgments. I provide unconditional acceptance to my suffering patients, strive to be a force for love to my partner, and offer my children all of the unconditional nurturing they deserve.

Then there's kink——transformation kink. In this container, I can spew out every name in the book, inflict pleasure and pain, let go of the nice girl image that's taken years off my life, and adopt a persona who doesn't give a shit in a way that balances my very respectable life with joy and excitement. *I cannot celebrate this win hard enough* because there was a very different time when I felt so lost and broken.

One night, nine months pregnant as a medical resident, I found myself on my knees. Again. In dramatic *Eat Pray Love* style, I looked up and begged for help from anyone, anywhere. I felt so alone—so completely despondent and exhausted that all I could do was drop to my knees and ask for guidance. Looking back, I don't know why I felt so bad. I had a promising medical career ahead of me, a loving and committed marriage and two gorgeous girls ages five and three, with a healthy baby boy on the way. We lived in the perfect starter home with the perfect SUV that fit three car seats. I checked off all my aspirations and *should have* felt the pride of success. Yet, night after night, I crumbled to my knees and prayed, *Please, give me a sign. I don't know why I feel so hopeless. Please just let me know I'm not alone. Please walk with me through this.*

That's when I found *Mama Gena's School of Womanly Arts: Using the Power of Pleasure to Have Your Way with the World* by Regena Thomashauer. This book would be my path to liberation and happiness. Using it as a guide, I engaged in a series of pleasure practices that made me feel quite silly and ridiculous at the time. For instance, I had fresh flowers delivered to myself with carefully crafted, loving self-addressed notes like, "You are such a hot, sexy, amazing mother. You are killing it!" I started wearing sparkly eyeshadow and intricate hoop-style earrings. Can you picture it? Remember, I was nine months pregnant and donned scrubs most of my waking hours. And I was not one of those cute, petite pregnant women. Since this was my third, I was enormous. Back-to-back pregnancies had long since buried what used to be my abs. But despite all that, I looked at my reflection each early morning and found a beautiful woman with sparkly bright eyes and decorated ear lobes. I felt a light shining through my eyes in a way that had been missing. I became as dedicated a student to the School of Pleasure as I was to my medical studies. Finally, I had a sense of perspective on who I'd been and who I was meant to become.

Throughout my personal healing and development path, I've remained determined and dedicated to reclaiming myself through pleasure and sexual expansion. I've gone to pussy decorating parties in New York City—each of which resulted in several delightful days of glitter and sparkles adorning my sheets. I attended sacred dancing and ceremonies with sister goddesses at a life-changing event in Mexico. I delved into my Erotic Blueprints™ throughout courses by master embodied healers. I writhed and cried as the journey along a somatic map on my body led me back home to my essence—something that felt completely lost but that I later learned can never really be.

The next step in my awakening was realizing my two parts needed to coexist. My animal (a.k.a. my inner goddess, the persona only allowed to come out on nights and weekends) refused to be caged, having tasted the satisfaction of embodiment. And I couldn't completely abandon who I was meant to be, a physician and momma of three. But I could remove the barrier to true happiness in both roles: constantly striving to be loved and accepted by being seen as good and nice. It was time to alchemize that society-taught character flaw. And ironically, a worldwide pandemic was about to provide the perfect testing ground to determine what I was actually willing to do to be fully embodied and experience joy.

In March of 2020, with COVID threatening to change the practice of medicine, I had just left the hospital floor. The medical director called an emergency meeting, and in 60 minutes, I was told every fact of this new virus. We were in New York, away from the epicenter of the China-born disease that quickly spread to the Western Hemisphere. We had protocols in place for many exotic, deadly diseases, such as SARS and Ebola. Our infectious disease specialist assured us as we prepared, and a leadership team (Command Center) was available for questions.

Three days later saw multiple cases of COVID-19, along with an "up and ready" status of the COVID ward we thought we had weeks to build. The medical director started posting videos meant to be reassuring, how wearing a simple gown and surgical mask was all that was needed for protection and that new diagnostic tests and treatments were already being researched. The next day, all of the hospital antibacterial soaps were inexplicably removed, and the masks were taken out of the supply shelves in the name of somehow reducing panic. A few of the hospital consultants came in with their own N95 masks and gave out a few to wear and reuse. I felt this fear in the pit of my stomach. I handled many difficult, life-threatening scenarios, but nothing that felt like this.

I returned to work a week later, and half of my colleagues were out ill or due to exposure to COVID. I asked logical questions: Where are the masks? What are we to do if we get sick? Almost overnight, the surgical team and ORs, consultants, and hospital administrators began working from home. I was left in my newly-named role of "frontline doctor" with nurses, aides, and soon-to-be travelers for hazard pay to care for COVID patients. Testing kits were hard to come by, labs were overrun with week-long waiting times, and treatment protocols changed daily. I admitted whole nursing home floors at once, very few of whom would return. There was a strict no visitor policy, and many died with just myself and a nurse saying goodbyes to the family via FaceTime from our cell phones. I dressed in scrubs, left in socks, and changed into my outside work shoes, an outside face mask, and a plastic bag for my hospital ID, driver's license, and credit card. I stopped eating at work as there was no time, and being maskless was too risky. I remember looking at my face with a jumpsuit, full face shield, hairnet, shoe booties, and double face mask with lines etched into my face, thinking: *How did I get here? Why am I still doing this? Will this sacrifice be worth it?*

On my path through medical school, my innate desire to serve at the highest level was slowly and insidiously replaced by the code of the toxic, modern doctor. I remember sitting in resident orientation and learning this common mantra every student doctor knows: Arriving early is on time; arriving on time is late, and arriving late is unacceptable. As my training went on, the list of unacceptable human characteristics and behaviors grew:

- Never complain about the need to rest, eat, or urinate.
- Always stand at attention as long as your attending stands.
- Since mistakes could cost a human life, perfection is expected.
- Time outside the hospital is wasted training time.
- If you don't see it as a trainee, you'll miss a new presentation of a common disease or an opportunity to see a rare disease. And if you don't see it, you won't be able to diagnose it.

In light of all this immense pressure, one of the strategies advised to me as a female physician—in the face of gender bias, including nurse animosity and the perennial boys club—was to be nice. More specifically:

- Ask about everyone's day.
- Buy lunch.
- Offer to do more than anyone else.

As the theory goes, if I worked hard enough at being nice, perhaps my true worth would be recognized. Yet somehow, as hard as I tried, I never seemed to be nice enough to get the worthiness and respect afforded to male physician counterparts. I felt overworked, overlooked, and continually exhausted. I trained myself not to speak up (a definite not nice no-no). I wasn't good at setting boundaries since that felt selfish. In fact, my entire identity became equated with over-giving: the world deserved all my gifts, but there was absolutely no room at all for my desires.

In Zen Buddhism, koan are the unanswerable questions of life. Every human can trace their human development to their related koan, a unique paradoxical question designed specifically for them. The value of one's koan is in the asking, searching, and never quite finding the solution. Therein lies the perfectly individualized path, with immaculately placed villains and mentors along the way. To that end, this has been my koan: Can I be a fully embodied human, designed for joy and pleasure, in a system that prides itself on detachment, overwork, and self-sacrifice?

This toxic medical culture promotes those who shed their human needs and, in the process, part of their heart and soul. It stigmatizes those who cannot "give from an empty well" and are (ironically) unable to turn off the very humanity that led them to this career path. In my journey, I might have been able to conform, except that I dared to have competing priorities: I became a mother before a doctor. I refused to sacrifice the compassion, care, and humanness my family needed. That decision led to my being labeled as "unprofessional" and my dedication to medicine ceremoniously questioned throughout years of training. Yet again, I unsuccessfully attempted to fit the round peg in a square hole. And yet, it was by rejecting the "niceness" foisted on me that I finally attained the emergence of a strange new heartfelt quality: kindness.

By way of distinction, kindness evokes a full heart pounding in my chest. At the same time, it embodies both a certain innocence and a conscious choice to hold myself and others to a higher standard. Kindness brings me back to the joy I felt as a second-grader who finished Elizabeth Blackwell's autobiography and thought: *Wait, I can do that.* I could hold the suffering, teach them the ingenious design of the human body, and learn how to heal sickness and disease. I was ready to sign up even before exploring a career in medicine in high school when I learned I'd not only get to be a member of such a respected and noble profession but also get paid very well. I repeatedly chose this profession because I cannot imagine a calling that equally satisfies my intellectual curiosity and a heartfelt desire to care for other humans in moments of illness. Because of what I've seen on a daily basis, I've developed wisdom that comes from an intimate relationship with the sanctity of death. I have learned—and passed along—a profound respect for the human body and how to take care of it. And I'm honored to have held my patients with such love and caring (notice I didn't say niceness) as they've faced difficult decisions and losses offered by the human experience.

The path I walk through these hospital halls is one of kindness, the new standard I've chosen for being a doctor. I embody kindness by modeling it: I nourish myself, take breaks. and have even learned to rest. From this place of self-care, I allow and encourage others to be human. I'm more compassionate and connected as a doctor to the therapeutic relationship I have with the patients whom I get to care for. Lastly, I'm free from the saccharine version of niceness still afflicting many of my colleagues. I let others be imperfect, make mistakes, and be humans with messy emotions. First, I give permission to myself and then freely to others, working to bring humanity back to the doctors so we can authentically infuse the healing process with kindness. And in the process, drive a stake right through the heart of niceness.

THE PRACTICE

A history of overvaluing and over-identifying with being nice has made it tough to say no–and even more difficult to detect what "no" *feels* like in your body. As the story goes, centering your own needs is seen as selfish. Requesting something from others codes you as being high maintenance. And conversely, if you were to sit with the discomfort of others resulting from your choices, it would feel like death. And yet the antidote is simple: the immediate death of your inner niceness. By learning to lovingly let go of these misguided codes from your past, you can uncover your genuine kindness. And it starts with finding where authentic "No" lives in your body.

Step 1: Standing Up Strong

Adopt a powerful stance with your legs slightly wider than your hips. Mindfully ground yourself into the current moment. Feel the fullness of your inhale and exhale. Be aware of your present thoughts. Focus on emotions you feel right now–remembering numbness is an emotion. Lastly, give attention to the sensations happening in your body. Some examples might include pounding in your chest, tension in your shoulders, tingling in your legs, or a pulsating in your abdomen.

Step 2: Creating Safety in Your Body

If this skill is new, this part of the tool may be all of the exercise you can or need to do initially. Slow your breathing and remind your body that you're safe. Assure your nervous system that you're not going to push yourself further than you need to and will only pursue your own growth edge. Now deeply envision being held in safety–perhaps based on a favorite item, place, or memory. With that in mind, adopt a picture of mountains holding your spine straight up with tangles of vines slowly wrapping around your legs and lower body. This allows you to be effortlessly held upright. Come back to this step and image as often as you need to. But it's very important to only proceed to the next step once you've achieved this sense of safety.

Step 3: Finding Your No

From this place of safety, scan your body to find where your "No" lives. Hint: Don't expect a giant red stop sign. Remember, it's been squashed and silenced for years. Expect a more quiet, subtle voice. When you recognize it, associate an image that fits. Maybe it's a shape, color, feeling, an animal, or even a younger version of yourself. Whatever it is, the goal is to find a representative image with which you can connect and converse. This part requires some practice and may feel awkward at first.

In case you find yourself wondering whether you're doing it right, you are. But if you're having difficulty accessing this part of yourself, try to hone in on it by turning up the feeling of your "No" to a ten. Ask yourself: What am I a no to? What do I no longer want to experience? What do I absolutely refuse to tolerate? Trust in the process and let yourself be guided by whatever memories and images arise. Be patient with yourself. Even if you sense your "No," it will take time to feel it completely.

If at any point this begins to feel like too much, go back to Step 2 and return yourself to safety. After all, this is an exercise meant to help facilitate emotional healing. I highly recommend using images unrelated to trauma you've experienced, especially if you haven't ever done any trauma healing work. Go for images that get you to a five, at least to start.

Step 4: Amplification

Give yourself a somatic expression of this "No" in your body. This may involve kicking or punching while screaming, "No!" Or something more demonstrative, like raising your hands above your head and authoritatively commanding, "No. I will no longer. . ." Spend as much time as you need and/or desire here. Don't be afraid to really let loose in this embodiment.

Step 5: Regulation

You may very well be feeling more—and bigger—"No" feelings than ever before. Place your hands on the part of your body that needs this powerful, fully expressed, authentic "No" energy. Take two to three minutes to breathe deeply in this place as a celebration for finding and expressing your "No" so bravely and so well.

Step 6: Integration

Who is this new version of you, expressing "No" in such bold ways? What is this person capable of creating? How does this person wake up? What will you wear? How will you nourish yourself, move your body, and carry yourself in the world? What types of intimacy or partnership are possible? How do you serve in your work and act in leadership? This is the "harvesting" of the work, so take the time to soak in the pride and gratitude with this part.

Congratulations, you did it! Although this exercise seems simple, it's not at all easy.

By fully expressing your conditioned "No," you'll make space for embodying the expression of your authentic, kind self and, in doing so, step into a bigger version of you than previously possible.

After surviving the frying pan of residency and jumping into the fire as a new attending right in the thick of COVID, **Dr. Lisa Tharler,** DO, MPH, manifested her dream job as a rural hospitalist at a critical care access community hospital in Hawaii.

On the Big Island, this board-certified internal medicine and pediatrics doctor is privileged to work with the indigenous Hawaiian community and her Ohana (family/team) of colleagues, nurses, and therapists. Tharler's dual masters in both Western public health and traditional Chinese herbal medicine and acupuncture allow her to holistically incorporate advocacy for marginalized communities along with cultural and indigenous healing practices. Post-COVID, she has become a trauma-informed, ICF-certified somatic coach for physicians who seek emotional mastery. This includes rewiring nervous systems away from the repetitive dehumanization historically taught in the medical training system by integrating breathwork, internal family systems (IFS), emotional freedom technique (EFT) tapping, and neuro-linguistic programming (NLP).

Using this powerful approach, she leads physicians through understanding and emotionally alchemizing the unconscious coding of niceness, self-sacrifice, and overwork that produces exhaustion, burnout, resentment, work dissatisfaction, and toxic family patterns. By rewriting the messaging leading to limiting beliefs and reclaiming the true healer within, physicians move beyond work and personal traumas to fully experience joy, playfulness, intimacy, and love. Ultimately, Dr. Tharler's goal is to redefine what a doctor/leader is and how embodying authentic kindness (for ourselves, patients, and others) can lead to satisfaction inside and outside the hospital.

In addition to just relaxing at home and gazing out at the cliffs overlooking Waipio Valley on Hawaii's northern coast, Dr. Tharler enjoys exploring, hiking, learning to paddleboard, and trying new instapot recipes with her three adorable children.

Visit http://linktr.ee/a2dl for related links and contact info.

CHAPTER 19

THE AWAKENED COUPLE

AN EMBODIED, SEXY APPROACH TO RELATIONSHIPS

Dr. Matt Helm and Larissa Czuchnowsky, MA

"Ending relationship struggles is only one choice away."

~Matt and Larissa

Matt: Have you ever tried to change your partner to get what you thought you needed and wanted? And at the same time thought, *If only my partner were different, we would be happier?* Have you ever been betrayed? Ever betrayed your true self? Have you hidden your feelings from your partner, afraid they couldn't handle it? Been in a lifeless relationship? Ever been on your knees, shattered from the grief and loss of a relationship ending? Do you find yourself repeating the same patterns with different people? We can all say yes to one, if not all, of these questions! We all know how difficult relationships are and how wonderful they can be.

Currently, Larissa and I are together only because we decided to dive in and use the mess of relationships to awaken us. We examined our shadow, transformed our trauma, and in the process, we found out that moving from relationship struggles to thriving is only one choice away. And we want to share how to use this choice to awaken and shift from misery to magic.

OUR STORY

The late sun was high above the river as I sipped my lemonade on the café patio; the rippling light shone brightly in my eyes. The town was alive with the sounds of people enjoying the summer evening. As I waited to meet my date for the first time, my hands were a little sweaty, but I felt calm. We had our first conversation the week before, and it left me feeling hopeful and optimistic. I looked at my phone for the time, and as I raised my head back up, a flash of a green dress came into view. It was worn by a gorgeous goddess of a woman smiling radiantly, and she was walking in my direction.

Wow, I said to myself as I took a deep breath. *This is not a usual date. This is special.*

She strolled over and said, "You must be Matt," with a friendly, open, and confident gaze.

"Yes. Hello Larissa. It's a pleasure to meet you in person! Why don't we go inside and get you something to drink?"

Little did I know that I had just met my future wife.

We talked all evening, and at one point during our wide-ranging conversation, she summed things up:

"What if problems weren't problems?" she queried. "What if reality was just the way it was, and our story about it was the problem?"

Yes, I thought to myself, *This is my type of woman!*

I stared intently into her eyes, and she looked into mine. What happened next, I will remember forever. We stopped all motion and caught each other in silent presence, riding a wave into timeless communion, open space, and oneness, surrendered together.

I couldn't speak.

Something sacred was happening as we attuned to each other, something beyond words.

I leaned over, and my lips brushed hers. At that moment, I knew our meeting was a destiny of sorts, a date for up-leveling and evolution.

I came out of that delicious kiss and thought, *I've met my match. I've found her. She is the one.*

Though this sounds idyllic, and it was, that meeting was preceded by our previous marriages, one ending in painful divorce and the other in death from cancer. We are together only because we decided to do something different with our heartbreak and loss and up-level through it. We used our pain to wake up, heal up, and show up to life and ourselves with radical honesty.

We've spent thousands of hours on the meditation cushion, in psychotherapy, on healing retreats, working with the best relationship experts, in coaching programs, and working with shamans.

We used the mess and excruciating pain to crack us open into being something else and to stop believing the old stories that kept us stuck in unhappiness and blame.

We wanted to thrive in our next relationships, ones that supported our evolution.

And now, we are living out our wisdom by using conflict as fuel for deeper authenticity, intimacy, and passion.

The **kindest** *thing you can do for your partner is to wake up. The best thing to do for your children is to wake up. The problem you think you're having in your relationship is not them; there is something inside of you that is struggling.*

*

Romantic Love delivers us into the passionate arms of someone who will ultimately trigger the same frustrations we had with our parents, but for the best possible reason! Doing so brings our childhood wounds to the surface so they can be healed.

~Harville Hendrix

Larissa: After enjoying the reflection of one's best self in your partner's eyes, all couples come to the inevitable place where core wounds and traumas get touched and triggered, and shadow parts (the exiled identities from childhood that we judge and lock away) come out to be seen and healed. This is the sacred work of the partnership. No one else but your partner can offer you this window into where you get stuck, where you back away, and where you shut down in hurt. Conflict with your partner shows you what needs to be released to be the best version of yourself. As seen from this reframing, conflicts are a gift, food for intimacy, and fuel for exponential growth.

Three years later. . .The Unexpected Birthday Gift

Larissa: It was my birthday, and as parents of two households, some days Matt and I can't be together. We prioritize our children whether we are together or apart, and this week, I was sad that my birthday fell at a time when Matt and I couldn't be together.

I am missing Matt, I thought. *It's not the same without him.*

The previous days were full of business deadlines and children's challenges. And we were both spent. The night before my birthday, we had a moment of conflict. Matt had clients all day, and I was excited to share some personal insights and was waiting for him to be available.

"I am just so tired, babe," he said. "I need to shut it off. Can we continue this conversation later?"

My heart hurt hearing those words. I noticed myself backing away and shutting down. *I've been waiting all day to share this with him. I'm so disappointed and don't know if I want to share with him anymore.*

We eventually made our way to deeply sharing our feelings, but we weren't together in person to fully resolve the tension and harmonize the energy through physical touch and contact.

The next morning, Matt called to celebrate my birthday.

"Happy Birthday, my queen! What's your highest and brightest intention for this beautiful day?" he asked.

I filled him in on the morning's happenings, the sweet surprises from my children (that he helped prepare), and my intention for the new year.

"Beautiful, I'm so happy to hear this," Matt said.

When I asked about his morning, he excitedly shared some guidance he received from a coaching friend. He began to list all the amazing things going on in his life since they started working together.

Whoa! What did he just say? My chest started to tighten. The heat started to build up inside me; I was triggered and started to get flooded.

Wait a minute, what does he mean? We've been working on these projects together for months. How can he suddenly say that his life is better because of his work with someone else? How can he say it right now, on my birthday?

The more I thought about it, the more upset I became. My mind seemed to have a will of its own and rampaged on. I felt so unseen. It touched old patterns of feeling unrecognized, over-functioning, and made me want to pull back and shut down.

It was hard to get words out.

"Well, Matt," I eventually said, "I feel like I need to focus on myself more and investigate how I've been doing too much. I've spent all this time on our project, our writing, and working through issues with our children, and you're giving all the credit to your coaching exchange. Maybe I just need to focus more on myself."

"Wait a minute Larissa," he responded, "I hear you're upset. I give to our kids and our projects too. And now you're pulling away from me and making up a story for why you are. It doesn't feel good. I was just sharing my excitement. And it makes me question what I'm doing and if I need to focus on myself more too. I wanted to celebrate you on your birthday. This isn't what I expected."

Silence. I could feel Matt start to shut down.

"Matt, now you're pulling away. We are both triggered. This *is* unexpected and uncomfortable. I know it's revealing something to me about my old stories, and it sounds like it is for you too. Let's take a break. I need to feel my way into what's going on and why I'm so triggered."

(Triggered is having an emotional reaction to an external stimulus that quickly engages the mammalian survival brain and the "fight, flight, freeze, and fawn response." When triggered, the brain releases a variety of chemicals leading to flooding and unconscious survival mode as the rational brain turns off.)

I felt a sickening fear. When we come to inevitable conflict, even though we always work through it, I feel afraid I'll lose him, that he won't like what I have to say, and that he'll decide to leave. It takes so much courage for me to stay with the truth of my feelings because I tend to get scared, accommodate, suppress my truth, and then feel resentful.

"Yes, I'm getting to where I'm shutting down," he said. "I don't like this; I wanted your birthday to be different."

"Yeah," I said. "It's hard for me to get out of this hurt too. But I appreciate this opportunity to let go of something here. Let's talk later."

"Okay."

We hung up.

Do you know this place of shutdown? When you're in a prison of hurt, and you want to get out, but you don't know how? When you want their arms around you, but you have just pushed them away and don't know how to shrink the distance between you? When it feels so hard to release your position once you're in it?

THE COMMITMENT TO BEING AWAKE AND AT THE STEERING WHEEL OF YOUR LIFE

"Until you make the unconscious conscious, it will dictate your life and you will call it fate."

~Carl Jung

Matt: Most struggle comes from a belief in something that isn't true. In the previous situation, we were closing down on a story, an old filter/conditioning/program from the past that didn't have anything to do with our partner at the moment. I was triggered and felt like I was wrong, my efforts unseen, and I felt like I ruined her birthday. My shadow parts emerged, and I felt anger, guilt, and even shame.

Larissa: It's painful to go to that place before the shutdown, to feel the trigger—the jealousy and the "security" I feel from engrained over-functioning (he'll need me and won't leave) and codependent tendencies. It was so uncomfortable, but I committed to sitting in the struggle, releasing old feelings, and choosing who I wanted to be next. This included the courage to reveal my story to Matt, as I had shame around feeling the way that I did. (Shame gets instilled when our caregivers don't meet our needs as children and we think it's because there is something wrong with us— instead of that our parents are busy, stressed, or in their own trauma).

Matt: After we each revealed what we usually keep locked away and hidden, guess what? We couldn't keep our hands off each other! We couldn't help but feel such love and gratitude for each other. We broke an internal prison bar together and had more energy available inside because of it. *We went from misery to magic.*

Want to hear a strange and true story? Most couples are living some form of this lie every day. The problem is that couples end up divorcing or ending their relationship because they are asleep and believe that their pain and dissatisfaction have to do with the external world (their partner or child.) They don't realize it's because of their internal world (that part of you created for survival in a moment of trauma, pain, hurt, or unmet need). When you are in these shadow parts and don't know how to stop, struggle, and surrender, you hurt each other and create a severe rupture in the relationship. When you don't wake up, you have a half-ass marriage that might look great on the surface but is miserable, lackluster, and on its way to ending.

It's important you come to know your inner reality and the beliefs, values, and ideas that operate behind the scenes. They're old and woven into your nervous and subconscious memory systems. It's easy to fall into your unconscious patterns of fighting for control, acquiescing, letting go of your needs, or dissociating. Until you bring all of these to the surface and make them conscious, they'll unconsciously dictate your love, sex, and relationship life. It's *a revolutionary struggle* to wake up. And it's the path to true freedom and joy and indeed to **embodying kindness.** Your relationship is the perfect place to make this struggle.

THE PRACTICE

HOW TO MANAGE EMOTIONAL TRIGGERS AND FLOODING: A FOUR-STEP FRAMEWORK

Matt and Larissa: One of the greatest killers of relationships is the belief that the problem you're having in your relationship is your partner, while your partner may be behaving in ways that are triggering you. What is more important is understanding the trigger. You're going to run into triggers, so accept them. The next step is to embrace them as your opportunity to let go of your unhealed and unconscious baggage. Here is the payoff: the energy you've tied up in fighting old battles can release into more love and enjoyment in your relationships. Here's a tool for working with your triggers, for turning *misery into magic:*

1. **Stop:** The moment you recognize you've been triggered, stop, and mindfully stop the narrative and stories you're beginning to tell yourself. As happiness researcher Dan Baker has found, you only have about a quarter second to stop emotional flooding from occurring. To do this, stay with your breath or choose to take a break. You can consciously stop the downward spiral by choosing to be in the moment. Your core wounds, traumas, and shadow parts all have unconscious stories and beliefs attached to them. When believed and projected onto your partner, these stories can have devastating effects on your relationships.

    Stop. Become a witness to the feelings, thoughts, images, and body sensations that have emerged.

2. **Stay, Struggle, Surrender:** If emotional flooding occurs, don't fight your feelings. Instead, stay with them and awaken. Notice your body's behavioral tendencies to shut down, dissociate, fight, acquiesce, or run away. It's uncomfortable to feel the discomfort and follow the thread to your core wounding. You may not want to feel this, but it is essential for your healing. This is like turning the light on in a dark room of your subconscious. Surrender. Don't move. Feel your feelings fully. Especially guard against spiraling into deeper stories, going further into your head: instead, focus on your

body. Is there a part of you that feels tighter or warmer? You are being offered an opportunity for healing, to live so entirely within the present moment as to allow the past to lose its control, allowing for your authentic self to emerge. Commit to yourself. Commit to surrendering to the present moment.

3. **State:** State your feelings to your partner. "I'm triggered, I'm distancing myself, I can't get out of this space. I don't want to talk." Depending on your state of consciousness and degree of triggering, an advanced option would also be to offer appreciation and gratitude. "I appreciate that you're bringing this part of me up for healing. This wouldn't be happening without you, even though it feels like shit. I'm grateful. I need 20 minutes."

4. **Select and Take Action:** After staying with the struggle, allow suppressed feelings to come up and be felt, experienced, and released. We enter a space where choice becomes possible. "Who am I beyond this pain, beyond this pattern? What is my highest intention for my growth and healing? What do I need for, and what do I need from my partner?"

    There is an opportunity for you to un-velcro from your past programming and conditioning. Who do you want to be with your partner? What is your new narrative? Select who you want to be and how you want to show up. At this stage, you begin to absorb and embody your truth. There is an opportunity to begin to move in the world in a new way.

When a couple chooses to be awake in life, their relationships thrive and can be extraordinary healing and fulfilling beyond words. It's sexy as hell to embrace your authenticity with your partner. You being free is your greatest wealth when it comes to relationships. Do you have the courage to remain awake, to free yourself from the prison of your unconscious beliefs, your trauma? To befriend and even love your hidden parts? It's the **kindest** thing you can do.

You don't need to struggle for years, get divorced, or end your relationship. What we have found is this. It only takes one of you to decide to do your inner work. All your relationships will be transformed if you do. Ending relationship struggle is just one choice away. We can't wait to hear how it goes!

If you would love more guidance and support on relationships, love, intimacy, or sex, please head over to https://www.relationshipsthrive.org. Let us help you thrive in relationships and turn misery into magic.

Dr. Matt Helm and **Larissa Czuchnowsky,** MA, are CEOs of Relationships Thrive, where they share relationship expertise on love, sex, parenting, wealth, and more. They have over 60 years of combined experience in coaching, therapy, business, leadership, and education. They are committed to relationships thriving! They hold certifications, licensures, and specializations in therapy and hypnotherapy, Accelerated Evolution, Erotic Blueprints, Feminine Embodiment, Spiritual Intelligence, Health and Wellness, and Shamanic Ceremony Facilitation. They believe that freedom is the new wealth and truth is the new sexy.

They offer a new paradigm for relationships for the planet, which includes how to have extraordinary, sacred, sexy, committed relationships while at the same time saving failing marriages, relationships, and families from the trauma and heartbreak of divorce. Their mission is to help couples and singles have the relationships they crave and find the love they desire. They also help singles magnetize the partner of their dreams and enter relationships awake with the essential skills needed to thrive.

Matt and Larissa find pleasure in spending time with their five children, dancing on the beaches of Mexico, mountain hiking, exploring farm-fresh cuisine, learning from plants, and serving others.

They offer courses, relationship breakthrough retreats, VIP deep dives for singles and couples, and private 1-1 coaching.

Connect with Matt and Larissa:

Website: https://www.relationshipsthrive.org

Instagram: Relationshipsthrive

Facebook: Relationshipsthrive

CLOSING MEDITATION

Thank you. Sincerely. I am so incredibly grateful for however you landed exactly here. I believe you are in the right place at the right time. I hope you have felt welcomed into our homes, our workplaces, and our schools. I trust you have been inspired by the brave stories and guided by the practices to EmbodyKind, to further examine personal development, partnerships, parenting, leadership development, team building, self-care, student-care, and/or school care. With hope that this transformational movement might just spark a revolution in your body, mind, and soul.

EmbodyKind,

Kristi Trader, MS
Founder: EmbodyKind

ACKNOWLEDGMENTS & GRATITUDE

To my boys, you are my favorite people. You are my best teachers. I appreciate your interest in and patience with my work. I hope you've taken away that happiness at work is more important than any title or paycheck you will ever get. And, I hope my commitment to that through the years has helped you feel as though I have been committed to you before anything else.

To every co-author/co-star that committed to this journey and bravely shared their story. This book would not have been born without your spark, your energy, and your love. I am in awe of your courage. Thank you for your authenticity and vulnerability.

To our cover artist, Avé Veneklasen. Your art extends beyond shapes and colors and captures the human spirit. This journey with you was magical! Thank you for making this title come alive.

To our poet, Dominique Linden, your words beautifully encapsulate the essence of this collaborative work. Coming to know you has been perfection. Thank you for so wonderfully summarizing EmbodyKind.

To our publisher, Laura DiFranco, and all of her team at Brave Healer Productions, you're all badass! Brave stories are told because of your kind souls. Thank you for changing the world.

EmbodyKind,

Kristi Trader, MS
Founder: EmbodyKind

WORK WITH KRISTI

Personal and Relational Development

Kristi is especially known for the premise of her work: growing individuals and relationships. Clients can work with her one-on-one or with their partner(s). Her exclusive and extensive curriculum covers: personality preferences, purpose, barriers to progress, human design, Reiki, your genius, values, time, appreciation, expression, embodiment, relating (romantically, parent/caregiver, worker/supervisor), vision, needs, wants, presence, pleasure, awareness, meditation, ritual, the divine, and world peace.

Contact Kristi to work on personal development, your partnership, or parenting at KristiTrader.com/contact or info@KristiTrader.com

Workplace Engagement

Kristi works with organizations' most valuable resource—people! Studies show that life satisfaction is directly correlated to workplace engagement and happiness. When we tell and appreciate each other's unique stories and personality preferences, our understanding of and commitment to each other increases. We become more empathic, establishing more clear and compassionate communication. We become more capable of critical thinking and problem-solving. And, we demonstrate a more creative and innovative approach to our work, ultimately yielding greater accountability and results.

Contact Kristi to work on leadership development or team building at KristiTrader.com/contact or info@KristiTrader.com

Education and Community Building

Kristi provides an array of community-building services, though she is regularly teaching and training staff and students in schools across the United States and Guam. She does so in partnership with two organizations:

CollaborateEdu: provides evidenced-based trainings to support education professionals in self-care, student-care, and school care.

Community Matters: provides services to create schools and communities that are safe, welcoming, and inclusive.

Contact Kristi to work on bullying prevention, restorative practices, and/or staff care at KristiTrader.com/contact or info@KristiTrader.com.

CLIENTS KRISTI HAS WORKED FOR

ALBION
C O L L E G E

ANTHONY WILDER

BATTLE CREEK AREA
CHAMBER OF COMMERCE

COMMUNITY
MATTERS

FAMILY SERVICE
& CHILDREN'S AID

Flagstar

HENRY
FORD
HEALTH

HL7
International

Jackson
COLLEGE

Michigan Department of
Health and Human Services

MENLO
innovations

MICHIGAN
PHYSICIANS
SOCIETY, LLC

Mid-State Health Network

ROBIN HILLS FARM

South Central Human Resource
Management Association

Spring Arbor
UNIVERSITY

SUBSTANCE ABUSE COUNCIL

TORRANCE
LEARNING

U.S. Chamber of Commerce
Institute for Organization
Management

What People are Saying about Kristi

"Outstanding and skilled facilitator. She created an atmosphere in which all participants felt welcome and valued. Her engaging personality, sense of humor, genuine compassion, passionate leadership, and thorough knowledge created an attractive environment."

~Col. Eric Ely, Maintenance Group Commander, Air National Guard

"Great facilitator. She really engages everyone. You were always made to feel you were truly important. I walked away with lessons learned that I am using in my daily work and relationships."

~Joann Farnham, Scholarship Manager, Battle Creek Community Foundation

"Wonderful facilitator who brought genuine experiences and insight to the course and demonstrated genuine concern for participants. Exceptional!"

~Kat Olsen, Human Resource & Business Manager, Binder Park Zoo

"Awesome personality and method of integrating the information presented with activities to stimulate conversation and thought. Very informative and enlightening!"

~Capt. Rachel Kallenberg, Comptroller, Air National Guard

"Great content and useful tools. Very relevant. Everyone enjoys the facilitator's presentation style. Very engaging and team building."

~Amy Schultz, MD, Director of Prevention & Community Health, Allegiance Health

"Calm and easy manner. Willingness to go with the flow. Created a warm, safe environment where the participants felt free to share openly. Not sure the last time I saw a group where almost everyone participated without prompting. Truly amazing!"

~Mary Jane Mapes, President, The Aligned Leader Institute

"What a great day it was! You handled everything with skill, grace, and professionalism. Great job, and well done! I express my gratitude for the gift of your life and all the people you touch with your gracious spirit. It is a great pleasure to work with you. I respect your hard work and professionalism. And I am appreciative to have such a wonderful and competent woman bring such fun and life to our team."

~William Divane, Psy.D., Assistant Dean, Director of Counseling Services, Albion College

TAKE A COURSE WITH KRISTI

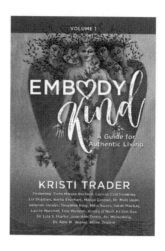

Kristi's course catalog is launching with the launch of this book, *EmbodyKind: A Guide to Authentic Living*. Each course will provide audio, visual, and/or audiovisual content to lead you through a self-paced revolution in your body, mind, and/or soul as it pertains to *EmbodyKind*.

The first course, EmbodyKind: Volume 1, will be a complement to this book in that it will provide tools to help you establish a foundation for future courses by:

- defining EmbodyKind and
- identifying your authentic self.

You can look forward to the content of some future courses including:

- Enhancing your self-image,
- Establishing trust in relationships,
- Increasing your commitment to and satisfaction at work, and
- Creating welcoming and safe communities, including in our schools through
- Bullying prevention and restorative practices.

Sign up at: KristiTrader.com/Courses

BE A CO-STAR IN MY NEXT COLLABORATIVE BOOKS

I am currently working with Brave Healer Productions to create other volumes of EmbodyKind. Each volume will expand on the space within which we are holding to practice EmbodyKind: home, work, and school.

At home, we are practicing personal development, partnerships, and parenting. At work, we are practicing leadership development and team building. And at school, we are practicing self-care, student-care, and school care, including bullying prevention, and restorative practices,.

If any of these spaces are familiar to you, if you practice within any of them, and if you have a story to tell, I would love to have you join us for the journey.

Each book requires a co-star to share their brave story and applicable practice that the reader can take away. Beyond writing, this opportunity invites you into a community that is changing the world. Authors have opportunities to participate in trainings, do podcast interviews, and join business development activities as part of the EmbodyKind and Brave Healer Production's family.

To explore opportunities to participate in my next volumes, contact me at KristiTrader.com/contact or info@KristiTrader.com

"Become an expression of love."

~Kristi Trader